THE WORLDS OF

HAYAO MIYAZAKI

For my mother
and father

THE WORLDS OF

HAYAO MIYAZAKI

The Influences and Inspiration
Behind the Iconic Films

Nicolas Rapold

F FRANCES
LINCOLN

CONTENTS

6

When I saw a Hayao Miyazaki movie for the first time, I immediately wanted to see all of them. And I also immediately wanted to talk to other people about my favourite scenes and moments, and to hear theirs. The main problem that many fans might have, in fact, is that Miyazaki hasn't made more movies, but inherent to them is that they reward repeat viewings to an unusual degree. His films are, as the title of this book suggests, worlds within our world; each has its own rules, sometimes the same as ours – here are children figuring out how to navigate the world – and often quite different, or even hard to understand, if it can be understood at all. But in *My Neighbor Totoro* (1988) or *Porco Rosso* (1992) or *Princess Mononoke* (1997) or *Spirited Away* (2001), Miyazaki knows that as long as these worlds move and feel with an internal consistency and emotional truth, they will hit home. And you *trust* these movies not to be false or trite, or ugly or tedious, for that matter.

The question this book hopes to explore is what goes into creating those worlds, which is not quite the same as explaining them. The transcendence – and the fun – of these movies very often eludes analysis. Miyazaki has a talent for not just pure invention but also assimilating his sources and inspirations until they become wholly his. In a beautiful way he has created his own cycle of modern myths with these films, fashioning characters and places that seem always to have existed, almost independently of origins or influences. Totoro is the most famous, and indeed emblematic, as the logo now of Studio Ghibli, the production house Miyazaki co-founded with fellow filmmaker Isao Takahata and former magazine editor Toshio Suzuki in 1985. But the same goes for an enduring character like the decent, overwhelmed, brave and resourceful Chihiro in *Spirited Away*, a film that bursts forth with something new on each viewing. New layers emerge with *The Wind Rises* (2013) or *Princess Mononoke*, too, yet without the films turning into fan fetish texts to be decoded: they are always alive and, like life, strange.

This book humbly seeks to share the inspirations and sources that help foster that sense of life in Miyazaki's films. That is why it begins with works of children's literature to reflect the sense of discovery with which Miyazaki instils the waking (and dreaming) moments of his films. The sense of entering a new world is common to Miyazaki and to these works, and like many of these books, his films are classics; they are not 'for children' but instead have a way of meeting you at your age – you grow with Miyazaki. His own biography emerges as inescapable in these movies, as a child of Second World War-era Japan, born into a world about to go up in flames, and as an adolescent and adult in the cultural and social ferment of postwar Japan. If Miyazaki could not meet the moment right away, working in television and film for others, he made up for it extravagantly later with worlds that contain multitudes.

Perhaps because of Miyazaki's early wartime upbringing, about half of his movies feel poised on the brink of destruction, and his first with characters wholly written by him, *Nausicaä of the Valley of the Wind* (1984), is the most extreme such example, set after one apocalypse and on the brink of a new one. His characters and settings are a melange of postwar daily life, historical amalgams and environments both infused with the beliefs of animism and threatened by the consequences of modernity. But whether the setting is the Muromachi Period of Japan or a legendary bathhouse for weary gods, the way these characters react to their circumstances, fantastical or factual, makes audiences feel recognized – especially if the struggles pose no obvious resolution.

Ambiguity is another hallmark of Miyazaki's films as they make their often dreamlike way through their narratives, zigging when you might think they'll zag, or simply ratcheting up the action derring-do in ways you had not thought possible. As a truly original voice, Miyazaki sometimes has fewer influences than counter-influences, as this book at times will argue: the urge to convey movement in a different way than conventional animation might, for example, or the desire to show nature as both beautiful and frightening at times, not a simple place to rope off and preserve. Peculiarly, to any movie fans who have seen their share of existential angst and dead time on screen, Miyazaki's ambiguities never feel like artistic gestures; we might reflect, but we aren't asked to interpret, only to look and to feel.

By any measure, Miyazaki belongs in the pantheon of visual stylists, which can partly be defined by those artists who not only do something as no one else quite could, but also do so in a way that shows or even expands the strengths specific to the medium. And Miyazaki is indeed very much the hands-on animator, making decisions on a minute level and sometimes desiring, it seems, to be able to draw an entire movie himself. Of course, he also excels at marshalling the team of talents necessary to create a Studio Ghibli feature film, who include background and colour designers who, with Miyazaki, help place these films in a lineage extending back to the woodcuts of Hokusai and other Japanese artists who have influenced others the world over.

By way of a roadmap, this book proceeds thematically through assorted influences, sources and contexts for the films Miyazaki has directed, offering multiple layers of detail and meaning but, one hopes, without demystifying their essential energy and appeal. 'If you try to explain it all within the film, the scale of the film shrinks,' Miyazaki said when confronted with explaining *Princess Mononoke* in full.[1] These pages aim to inform and, perhaps like a Miyazaki story, take the reader down unexpected and eccentric byways, but the ultimate goal is always to encourage more watching of the movies and, as Miyazaki would intend, of the world as well.

CHAPTER ONE

FOUR WAYS THROUGH THE LOOKING GLASS

How Four Great Writers Have
Inspired Miyazaki's Story-Building

Making an Entrance

Every Miyazaki movie is a portal to another world, and very often it's the story of a child who finds it just next door. A little girl will scurry through a thicket behind her house and find the cavernous haunt of a sleepy bear-like creature. A bereaving boy will notice a derelict tower nearby and squeeze through a crack to find a kingdom of birds and other beasts. A bored 10-year-old will cross a bridge to a bathhouse buzzing with both otherworldly and mundane activity.

All these are entry points in Miyazaki films, specifically a towering classic (*My Neighbor Totoro*), his acclaimed late-career fantasia (*The Boy and the Heron*, 2023), and his millennium-capping masterpiece (*Spirited Away*). Their sense of curiosity and the porousness of their realities share much with a rich tradition of adventure in children's literature, wherein girls and boys stumble upon or tumble into alternate universes of one sort or another. Miyazaki was long a voracious reader of books for the younger set, ever since being a self-described 'physically weak' child. He has championed titles that range across the school-age canon, notably leaning towards Western authors. In 2011, he even wrote a collection of essays on children's literature, evocatively titled *The Doorway to Books*, at the behest of a popular publisher in Japan.

Lewis Carroll (aka Charles Dodgson) is one such writer who looms on Miyazaki's list of inspirations, and generally in Japan, where his works have received numerous translations (not to mention theme restaurants and cosplay outfits). Carroll's *Alice's Adventures in Wonderland* (1865) begins with a mix of psychological and physical transport that finds immediate echoes in Miyazaki. Young Alice's journeys begin after she dozes off while her sister reads to her on a riverbank, and she chases after a white rabbit and falls down a hole. The rest is history, or modern myth, since Carroll's imagery feels almost as if it has always been with us. And Miyazaki's visual and narrative references to the book in *My Neighbor Totoro* are unmistakable. After scampering through the underbrush, pint-sized Mei falls, like Alice, down an earthy chute into another domain and later encounters a feline creature with the enigmatic piano-key grin of Carroll's Cheshire Cat.

Mei and her older sister, Satsuki, have recently moved to the countryside with their father, and they take to their musty old house with whirlwind gusto. Early on, Miyazaki establishes the slightly dreamlike bleed between worlds through the presence of sentient dust bunnies that haunt the nooks and crannies (called *susuwatari*, or 'wandering soot'). As with Alice's snoozy sighting of the white rabbit, Miyazaki is leaving open the initial possibility that Mei has dreamt up her foray into Totoro-land: indeed, Satsuki finds her sister sound asleep behind the bushes after her adventure. But in a Miyazaki movie, the possibility that what we've seen is a dream, or dream-related, is not grounds for disappointment that it wasn't real. It's confirmation of how real dreams are, and how expansive and deep their realms can be and feel.

↑ The Cheshire Cat sits on a tree branch in one of John Tenniel's 1865 illustrations for *Alice's Adventures in Wonderland*

↑ The Catbus, a unique mode of transport, perches in a tree with Mei and her older

↑ Mei pursues the strange being (Totoro)
that she encounters near her new house
in *My Neighbor Totoro*

↑ The heron stands inside the mysterious
tower that seems to bend space and time
in *The Boy and the Heron*

That's not to speak of Totoro or the Catbus as dreamlike hallucinations; they are more like forest spirits (*kami*) in line with traditions of animism. But they improve upon the whimsy of Carroll: Miyazaki's narratives have a dreamlike ease, shown in how they naturally introduce and incorporate new fantastical characters, and move forwards or sideways without the quest-driven single-mindedness that hamstrings so much contemporary commercial animation. Like Alice in Wonderland, Satsuki and Mei struggle to understand what rules or even tendencies govern the secret world to which they have gained access. But Miyazaki holds open the promise that instead of tyrannical tea parties or the Queen of Hearts, these two sisters can take part in and grow from the rituals they encounter, like the adorable dance Totoro and friends engage in to boost the plants in their family's backyard.

It's easy to forget that Totoro does not even appear on screen until 30 minutes into the film. *My Neighbor Totoro* is comparatively serene most of the time, full of the moments associated with the concept of *ma*, the rest points or negative space that complete the whole. If one can classify dreams according to kinds of sleep, Miyazaki channels the fanciful reverie of an untroubled nap, with playful Alice-like shifts in scale for Totoro and the Catbus, who expand and stretch and contract in size according to the demands of the situation. Talking of the sizable Totoro, Miyazaki once recalled the Japanese writer Kenji Miyazawa's 1924 story 'The Acorns and the Wildcat'. Reading the tale, he had imagined the wildcat, actually a forest magistrate, as 2m (6.6ft) tall, not the small creature shown in his edition's illustration, and it was this conception of its stature that made him love its world.

In Miyazaki's *The Boy and the Heron*, the mood is rather more like a recurring dream with a dose of fever: teeming, overwhelming, frantic, a resolution never quite in reach. That recalls, too, the frenzied pursuit aspect to *Alice's Adventures*, with its cavalcade of unpredictable, sometimes imperious, personalities who push her story this way and that, and weigh in on her progress. Like Satsuki and Mei, Mahito is a newcomer to the country, where his widowed father has resettled the family and remarried. Mahito is sad and irritable after the death of his mother, and so the film begins in a different key, but the narrative engine is similar: he's drawn into a fantastical other world by an interloping creature, in this case an enigmatic talking heron. There he discovers a host of inhabitants with distinctive worldviews (though perhaps less pernickety than those in Carroll's), including a strict royal regime of parakeets.

Not every Miyazaki film dramatizes a Carroll-like plunge into another world, and indeed his characters very often are moving back and forth between the other realm they discover and this one, as in *The Boy and the Heron*. But the vivid sprawl of his movies means that anyone stepping into a cinema (or giving oneself up to a screen at home) will be a bit like an Alice in finding a world with its own rules, aesthetics and even, in Miyazaki's constant return to images and machines of flight, physics. That total immersion evokes *Alice's Adventures* but also reflects the feelings of discovery and curiosity untainted by preconceptions that Miyazaki so clearly prizes in children's literature generally. Even his characters are besotted with books: sweetly enough, when Mei first returns from Totoro-land, she says it reminds her of the book about trolls that her mother read to her.

↑ Alice, larger than life, watches the rabbit scamper off in Tenniel's 1865 illustration for *Alice in Wonderland*

↑ Kenji Miyazawa, whose stories are classics of Japanese literature and influences on Miyazaki's fantasies

A Place to Heal

The two sisters in *My Neighbor Totoro* are a joyous pair, taking to their new house with gusto, but the wonder of their escapades exists in the shadow of the illness of their mother, who's away receiving treatment. Narratives of grief and of recovery from a mortal blow to the family unit form another pillar of Miyazaki's work. Sadness over an absent mother suffuses *The Boy and the Heron*, in which Mahito's mother dies in a burning hospital set alight during a 1943 firebombing. In *The Wind Rises*, the psychic burden shifts somewhat, as it's the wife of aircraft engineer Jiro who is ailing and ultimately passes away from a long-term case of tuberculosis. One gets the sense that all are variations on the trauma Miyazaki himself suffered when his mother spent nearly a decade battling spinal tuberculosis, starting when he was around six years old.

The Boy and the Heron is perhaps most closely drawn from these years in Miyazaki's childhood, with the death of the character's mother acting as a kind of purgative playing out of what he as a boy must have dreaded could happen. The personal history suggests that Miyazaki is at least partly in the category of an artist who is revisiting, probing, worrying at and weaving entire worlds around an emotional wound that never quite healed. One of the most famous such authors was C. S. Lewis, who wrote *The Chronicles of Narnia* in the 1950s. He described the effects of his mother's premature death when he was nine as if a continent had sunk, like Atlantis, leaving only sea and islands behind. It's possible to imagine the vast lands of Lewis's work or the teeming realms of Miyazaki's as a way of rebuilding and repopulating a lost world with life.

Lewis wrote the *Narnia* books in England shortly after the Second World War, during the very years when Miyazaki's mother was ill. Miyazaki's family left Tokyo for the countryside in 1944 to escape Allied bombings, and indeed the four sibling heroes of Lewis's work are evacuees to the English countryside, where they discover their magical wardrobe. Yet, despite their equivalently expansive menageries, Lewis's lands of magic and talking animals, with their good-and-evil frameworks, feel less akin to Miyazaki's mostly more ambivalent realms than the work of an earlier British-born writer, Frances Hodgson Burnett.

Miyazaki has specifically cited Burnett's *The Secret Garden*, published in 1911, as one of his favourite children's books, and its story of displacement and coping immediately strikes a chord: after the death of her parents from cholera, 10-year-old Mary is whisked away from India to Yorkshire, England, to live with an uncle. Like Alice in Wonderland or Mei stumbling across Totoro, Mary unlocks and accesses a neglected walled garden, where she eventually spends time tending flowers and where she brings her uncle's sheltered son (with the help of her maid's kindly brother). It's a children's classic that dwells on the need to heal and on how the world, for all its obstacles, can present ways for us to do so. It's like a ghost story but with the promise of coping with rather than being tormented by the ghost.

↑ C. S. Lewis, the British author of *The Chronicles of Narnia* (1950–56), whose mother's death left a lasting wound

↑ Frances Hodgson Burnett, who wrote *The Secret Garden*, the beloved 1911 novel about a child coping with grief

↥ Mahito runs to embrace Lady Himi, who might be an alternate-world version of his deceased mother in *The Boy and the Heron*

Burnett herself reeled from the death of one of her young sons for years, and her work offers an enduring promise of recovery and renewal (with its own extended lineage on stage and in cinema). Mahito, in *The Boy and the Heron*, is gravely in need of some way to process not only his mother's death but also his father's remarriage to his mother's sister in the unfamiliar environs of the countryside, after spending his early years (like Miyazaki) in Tokyo. The roses, violets and poppies of Burnett's garden seem to carry an almost magic potency, and for lonely Mahito, Miyazaki brings his full imaginative forces to bear in the world accessed through a derelict tower.

The heron tempts Mahito with the possibility of somehow reconnecting with his deceased mother, a fanciful prospect that might seem almost cruel to offer (and, indeed, Miyazaki's heron has an almost Carroll-esque streak of barbed whimsy). But the gravelly voiced bird – who it emerges is actually a goblin in disguise – is speaking a version of the truth. The world Mahito visits becomes, essentially, a place for meeting versions of people he knows and working through unresolved feelings by undertaking (sometimes inscrutable) challenges, not unlike how Mary's tending of the garden leads to her own regrowth. It's a pattern of regeneration that recurs throughout Miyazaki's secret worlds, which set up parallels between outer and inner journeys (to downright vertiginous extents in *Howl's Moving Castle*, adapted from another British author, Diana Wynne Jones).

That Miyazaki views this and other films as more than flights of fancy can be confirmed by the Japanese title of *The Boy and the Heron*, which is *How Do You Live?* The name comes from a novel by Genzaburo Yoshino about the sentimental education of a 15-year-old at school and at home, first published in 1937 and an avowed favourite of Miyazaki's, though the film is not an adaptation. In fact, Miyazaki's original proposal for filming *The Boy and the Heron* was based on *The Book of Lost Things* (2006) by John Connolly (which includes a blurb by Miyazaki in its Japanese edition). Connolly's book also centres on a boy whose mother dies (in 1939) and whose father relocates to the home of his new wife, and taps Burnett's regenerative tradition with a world accessible through a garden, via the assistance of a figure who appears in the boy's dreams.

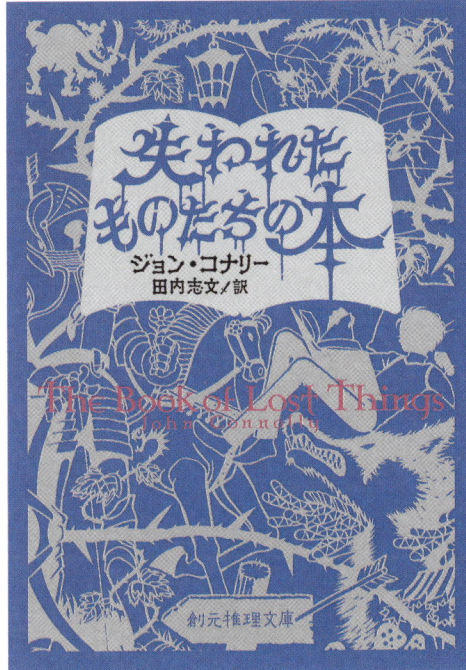

↑ The Japanese edition of *The Book of Lost Things* by John Connolly, the basis of Miyazaki's proposal for *The Boy and the Heron*

It's a narrative paradigm again familiar from Carroll's wonderlands, yet what clearly attracted Miyazaki is the robust emotional dynamic – almost consistently one of hope, often hard-won but distinct, and not reducible to a lesson. 'Liberated from reality and relaxed, viewers find themselves pulled into scenes showing the protagonists and a cartoon world and then may find that the experience evokes secret hopes and longings in themselves,' Miyazaki said in an interview with *Animage* magazine.[2] The details of *The Boy and the Heron*'s sometimes baffling gallery of characters – a helpful fisherman, puff-like spirits called *warawara* that recall the soot sprites of *My Neighbor Totoro*, a wizard reorganizing dimensions through a pile of symbolic blocks – seem less important than Miyazaki's creation of a place for psychological and even spiritual growth.

↑ Mahito rests at the base of a tree after joining forces with the enchanted heron in *The Boy and the Heron*

At Home in a Strange Land

Taking Fantasy on Its Own Terms

While *My Neighbor Totoro* and *The Boy and the Heron* show Miyazaki plunging characters into unfamiliar worlds, there's another narrative variation that's just as prominent in his work. Instead of the discoveries of strange realms that lead to growth and healing, a film like his *Nausicaä of the Valley of the Wind* presents a land that the characters inhabit and know quite well already, and a protagonist whose qualities appear inbuilt from the beginning, and are simply demonstrated on an ever-greater scale. The revelation occurs on the audience's part, learning the depth of Nausicaä's bravery and caring as she takes action.

In *Nausicaä of the Valley of the Wind*, Miyazaki envisions a postapocalyptic future, as many of his contemporaries did at the time, in which humans struggle to survive amid the threat of war and other disasters. Nausicaä, a princess, must save innocents from a horde of hulking insects called the Ohmu, whom she treats with unexpected compassion, and threats from the bellicose kingdom of Tolmekia and the mysterious Sea of Decay, which she sheds new light on for her beleaguered people. It's a story that Miyazaki had already begun telling in manga form a few years earlier, and, showing the tale's hold on him, he would continue and conclude this manga about a decade later.

Miyazaki's film of the future has its origins in ancient literature, as its title suggests. He first read of Nausicaä, one of the many exotic encounters in the journeys of Homer's *Odyssey*, not from the Greek work itself but from a popular collection of Greek mythological figures first published in 1975, *Gods, Demigods and Demons* by Bernard Evslin, who had his widest success writing for younger readers. Appearing in Book VI of Homer's epic as the daughter of King Alcinous and Queen Arete of the Phaeacians, Nausicaä shows her mettle when she greets a bedraggled, half-naked Odysseus who surprises her playing by a river. Her friends run off, but she stays and ultimately cares for the injured traveller, who attributes his survival to her before sailing off.

Charmed by this brave figure with a talent for singing, Miyazaki sought out a novelization of the *Odyssey* but he felt it watered down the lively character. Miyazaki's idea of Nausicaä would bring to his mind a Japanese heroine from an eleventh-century collection known as *Tales of the Tsutsumi Middle Counselor* (or alternately, 'The Riverside Middle Counselor'). The particular story that resonated is called 'The Lady Who Loved Insects', about an intelligent young noblewoman with a passion for studying caterpillars and other 'vermin' for hours rather than flowers and butterflies, despite the enormous pressures of the Heian Period to prepare for marriage and adhere to conventional costuming and hair. Nausicaä's genesis offers an example of two tendencies for Miyazaki: not just blending Western and Eastern influences, but also simply his perpetual hunger to improve upon and enliven subjects and characters that intrigue him.

↦
Poster for *Nausicaä of the Valley of the Wind*:
Princess Nausicaä with one of the Ohmu,
a tribe of formidable creatures

A HAYAO MIYAZAKI FILM   "NAUSICAA OF THE VALLEY OF THE WIND"   EXECUTIVE PRODUCERS YASUYOSHI TOKUMA MICHIO KONDO   ORIGINAL STORY AND
SCREENPLAY BY HAYAO MIYAZAKI MUSIC BY JOE HISAISHI   TOKUMA SHOTEN AND HAKUHODO PRESENT "NAUSICAA OF THE VALLEY OF THE WIND"
PRODUCED BY ISAO TAKAHATA DIRECTED BY HAYAO MIYAZAKI   ©1984 Nibariki · GH

Recalling his encounter with the eleventh-century text, Miyazaki's reaction to this shrewd bug enthusiast is a telling one: he wondered, simply, what would happen to her in such a society. Would she continue her independent streak, in defiance of stringent custom? It's possible, then, to think of Miyazaki's film concept as imagining what might come next for a Nausicaä-type character – what would self-realization look like for his princess, who, like his two pre-modern models for her, had already demonstrated strong character? When he began his foray into the world of Nausicaä in the form of manga, he had said he hoped to bring the young heroine 'into a world of peace and freedom' – with the sentiment of freedom also seeming to encompass her steadfast path.

In Miyazaki's film, Nausicaä, all of 16 years of age, must grapple with the nightmarish overarching narratives presented by the angry Ohmu and the fathomless Sea of Decay. One way of looking at her self-adopted role as a saviour for tribes weaker than the Tolmekia is finding a way of making all of these trajectories coexist: the tribes, the Ohmu (whom she pacifies by returning one of their lost offspring) and the Sea of Decay (a toxic dumping-ground that she demonstrates is actually part of an ancient system that has outlived its usefulness in a time of worsening crisis). Rather than a story of eccentric novelty or therapeutic escape, Miyazaki's world here is a place to be saved from ruin, and a kind of proving ground for engineering a resolution.

Nausicaä of the Valley of the Wind was the first original feature Miyazaki directed and wrote, leading the year after its release in 1984 to the founding of Studio Ghibli, the production house for *My Neighbor Totoro* and his subsequent films. He's plainly fond of Nausicaä – who starts impressively, a flying ace and friend to all, and ends even more impressively as something approaching a messiah figure – to the extent that one can sense an identification with her drive and self-realization. Even the wasteland that surrounds her in the film seems to dovetail with Miyazaki's dark misgivings about Japan's success at the time or about the road ahead for the modern world as a whole.

Yet even in detecting resonances within Miyazaki's narratives and characters with past works of literature and art, it's worth remembering the organic nature of his creative process. This he sometimes describes essentially as getting himself into jams and then figuring out solutions. *Nausicaä of the Valley of the Wind* might seem to culminate with supreme symbolism when our heroine is trampled to death and then brought back to life: bathed in golden light and floating through the sky, as people look on in awe, she resembles some kind of prophet. Yet when interviewed immediately after the film's release, Miyazaki was still fretting over these very images, saying he had explicitly intended to avoid any religious undertones. His storytelling seeks to sustain dramatic tension while retaining mystery, as he put it with regard to Nausicaä: not a quest but a story transpiring within 'a vastness that we might not fully understand'.[3]

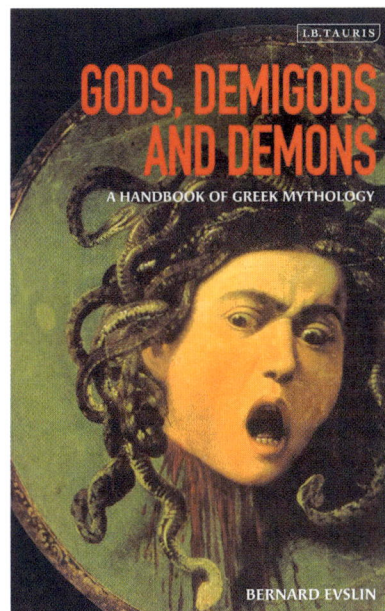

↑ *Gods, Demigods and Demons* by Bernard Evslin, a popular anthology through which Miyazaki learned about Nausicaä in Greek myth

Getting
There

Jules Verne and
Journeys Through
Technology

When Hayao Miyazaki studied economics at university, he also attended a children's literature study group. One of the books he read was *Twenty Thousand Leagues Under the Sea* (1870) by Jules Verne, whose adventures would prove to be another lodestar for the future animator's worlds. The ferment of the Industrial Revolution and its paradigm-shifting technological innovations (both explicitly industrial and otherwise) inspired the French writer to extrapolate fantastic voyages made possible by novel machinery, such as the submarine in *Twenty Thousand Leagues* or the flying craft of the 1886 novel *Robur the Conqueror* (also known as *The Clipper of the Clouds*), an epoch-bridging portmanteau invention resembling a ship with wings.

The flying machines and otherwise mobile contraptions in Miyazaki's worlds sometimes tend to get lumped in with steampunk, a futuristic vision featuring Victorian-era technology which was coined in the 1980s. But Verne provides both the heart and brains for the particular narrative drive that recurs in Miyazaki's films: individuals pushing into new frontiers with the help of innovative transport, whether the walking architectural assemblage of *Howl's Moving Castle* (2004), the fanciful Italian fighter plane of *Porco Rosso*, or the variety of Vernean airships cruising through *Laputa: Castle in the Sky* (1986). With their particular temperamental challenges, these machines require focus, expertise and risk-taking of their intrepid pilots to carry them through the story.

Flight is a well-established obsession of Miyazaki's, but the importance of Vernean motion to his stories is more than a matter of his aerodynamic obsession. Witness what Miyazaki taps into when he once described *Twenty Thousand Leagues* in an interview with two university professors for *Kikan Iichiko*: 'Jules Verne's story of going under the sea overlaps with entering into one's own internal world.'[4] The places to which Verne's submarine – and the Miyazaki's menagerie of machinery – take us, and the characters, are not merely physical or geographical, but psychological and even spiritual. Miyazaki may liberate himself from Verne's proudly scientific trappings, as shown especially by *Howl's Moving Castle* or *Kiki's Delivery Service* (1989), both rooted in magic, but there remains a palpable belief in transport, in every sense.

In Miyazaki's hands, Verne's sense of adventure can readily embrace an anarchic sense of fun, perhaps most riotously in *Laputa: Castle in the Sky*, which followed the doom-laden brinksmanship of *Nausicaä* and offered a sense of release. The first feature released under the Studio Ghibli banner was named after the levitating magnetically powered island described in Jonathan Swift's *Gulliver's Travels*, the 1726 work that anticipates Verne's free-flowing innovations but put in service of satire rather than science fiction. Swift's Laputa is populated by self-absorbed philosophers so distracted by music and mathematics that they don't notice the shoddy construction of their houses or the rampant adultery. (Oddly enough, Japan itself is one of the final stops on Gulliver's travels, and the only real one, visited when the shogunate still enforced isolation.)

↦
Jules Verne,
whose futuristic
nineteenth-century
works helped
inspire the fanciful
flying machines in
Miyazaki's work

↤
An 1886 engraving
illustrating an airship
from *Robur the Conqueror*
(aka *The Clipper of the
Clouds*) by Jules Verne

↑ The view from Earth looking at the floating
island of Laputa in *Gulliver's Travels*, in
J. J. Grandville's 1850 illustration

↑ A floating island from
Laputa: Castle in the Sky

↑ A diligent robot left behind on Laputa holds
heroes Pazu and Sheeta in *Castle in the Sky*

Swift's satire of the Enlightenment worship of reason is not taken up by Miyazaki. He seems more inspired by the satirist's outlandish imagination and wild sense of scale – Howl's moving castle could well be a Swiftian creation, were it played for allegory – rather than his often caustic commentary. But the flying castle by the name of Laputa does appear as a once-great abandoned empire in Miyazaki's *Castle in the Sky*. In his original proposal for the film, Miyazaki imagined Laputa as one part of a 'thrilling classic action film' intended for children of school age: the heroes are a boy, Pazu, from a mining town, and Sheeta, a girl with royal lineage, who in the film team up against a chaotic but shrewd band of air-pirates and a government agent, Muska, bent on infiltrating Laputa in a sinister power grab.

In his proposal Miyazaki called the setting 'vaguely European', and described the time period – with a characteristically deadpan description that is, intentionally or not, quite funny – as 'an era when machines are still exciting and enjoyable and science does not necessarily make people unhappy'. The line turns out to be apt, too, for Verne's approach to science as a vehicle for adventure and transformation, a sense of promise that transmutes into infectious fun in *Castle in the Sky*, though gradually shadowed by Muska's menace. Miyazaki also proposes featuring in the story an aircraft called an 'ornithopter' that will be an 'important character' in and of itself. The film's opening sequence parades a series of airships that evoke Verne's designs, or perhaps their iterations in Czech filmmaker Karel Zeman's 1958 live/stop-motion hybrid *Invention for Destruction*.

Yet the climax of *Castle in the Sky* demonstrates the limits and the particular contours of Miyazaki's interest in technologically boosted narratives. After Muska acquires power over Laputa's weapons of mass destruction, he soon moves to destroy his rebelling army's massive airship, the Goliath, and promises to attack humanity as a whole next. (Muska makes apparent reference to Indra's fiery lightning in the Hindu epic *Ramayana* – from the seventh to fifth centuries BCE – and Sheeta's name suggests that of Sita, the Hindu goddess who looms large in the *Ramayana*.) What potential Laputa may have had as a utopian bastion is abruptly put out of reach – Muska's explosion has nuclear echoes – and so Sheeta moves to hobble Laputa's weapon centre with a magic spell of destruction, which also sends Muska to his demise. The two young heroes then reunite with the loose-cannon air-pirates, who turn out to be inclined to the good, for a final farewell.

This ending is a departure from that of Swift's Laputa, which harbours an ineffectual society but is not destroyed. Yet it feels in keeping with Verne's faith in nature's balance and in its potential for freedom. 'The sea does not belong to despots,' Verne writes in *Twenty Thousand Leagues*, and in *Castle in the Sky* and elsewhere, one could imagine Miyazaki saying the same about his animated skies, where aircraft allow not just flights of fancy, but also freedom.

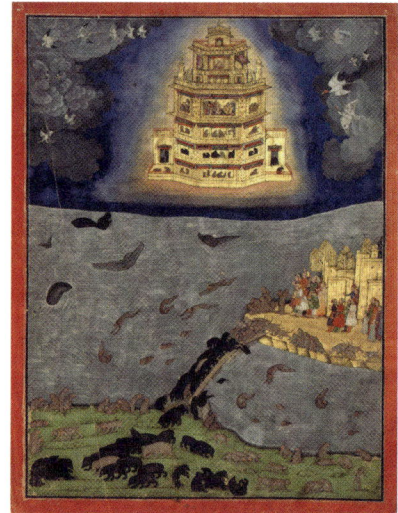

↑ A seventeenth-century illustration of a scene towards the end of the *Ramayana*, after the rescue of Sita, echoed in the name of the heroine in *Castle in the Sky*

↑ Nineteenth-century illustrations for the
work of Jules Verne: *Around the Moon*
(top left) and *Twenty Thousand Leagues
Under the Sea*

CHAPTER TWO

WE COULD BE HEROES

How Four More Writers Yielded Models
of Young Female Independence

Hardworking
Heroines

The Resilience of
Heidi and Kiki

On 16 July 1973, a 32-year-old Hayao Miyazaki travelled to Switzerland to visit the small town of Maienfeld. He was joined by his future partner at Studio Ghibli and director at the time, Isao Takahata, as well as the character designer Yōichi Kotabe and a producer, Junzō Nakajima. The group took pictures of the mountainous countryside and its hardy barnyard animals, popped into a souvenir shop at the Jungfraujoch glacier, posed for a picture at a farmer's cottage and toured the Johanna-Spyri-Museum. Spyri, in fact, inspired the trip through her novel *Heidi*, which was published in 1880 and has been reprinted and translated across the globe. Soon enough, this irrepressible avatar of the Swiss mountains was to become a star on Japanese television, subject of a 52-episode adaptation and a key part of Miyazaki's own imaginative travels.

Titled *Heidi, Girl of the Alps*, the 1974 series became a classic in its own right, inspiring fan bases in Japan and across the world in its assorted dubbed versions. Heidi shows an appealing resilience and decency as an orphan sent to live with her grumpy adoptive grandfather in the mountains, plus a stint with a family in Frankfurt overseen by the fearsome governess Fräulein Rottenmeier. Following an adaptation of Finnish author Tove Jansson's classic *Moomin* series, the hit *Heidi* programme confirmed the success possible by adapting children's literature, and inaugurated an annual animated series on Japanese television called *World Masterpiece Theatre* that ran for 25 more years and featured European locales.

Miyazaki served as the scene designer and layout artist on the *Heidi* series; it was properly the brainchild of Takahata, the director. But this Swiss-born character captured – and, in her animated form, truly embodied – the energy that distinguishes the many heroines in the features that Miyazaki later directed. With *Heidi*, Takahata sought to go beyond the formulas of either contemporary Japanese anime at the time or Disney for that matter, and portray a literary character with realism and substance – an ambition shared by Miyazaki. 'We wanted to provide the children watching our series something that would inspire joy, not just be cute, beautiful or fun,' Miyazaki said in a 1982 lecture.[5]

The animator had already been part of an abortive attempt to portray another literary heroine with an adaptation of *Pippi Longstocking*, the 1945 novel about a nine-year-old orphan who lives quite gloriously all by herself, written by Swedish author Astrid Lindgren. Miyazaki and company even travelled to Sweden for location scouting in 1971, visiting the island of Gotland and the castle town of Visby, and to secure Lindgren's blessing (which was not forthcoming). Pippi's signature red pigtails resurfaced later in the rampant locks of the wild-granny pirate leader in *Laputa: Castle in the Sky*. By comparison to Pippi, Heidi might seem a bit tame, but the joie de vivre of Spyri's character and the fresh-air vibrancy of the mountain landscapes are faithfully portrayed in the Japanese series.

↥ Johanna Spyri, the Swiss author of *Heidi*,
the 1880 classic about a girl growing up
in the Alps

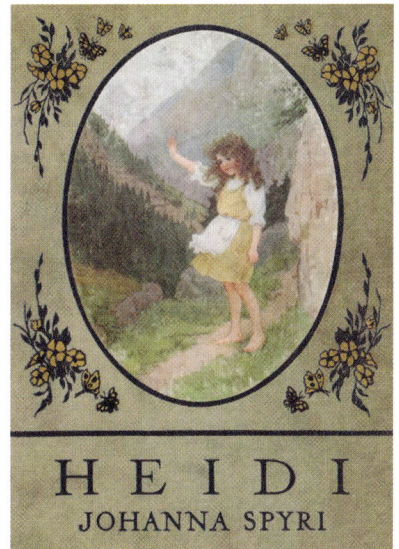

↥ Cover of an American edition of *Heidi* (1919)

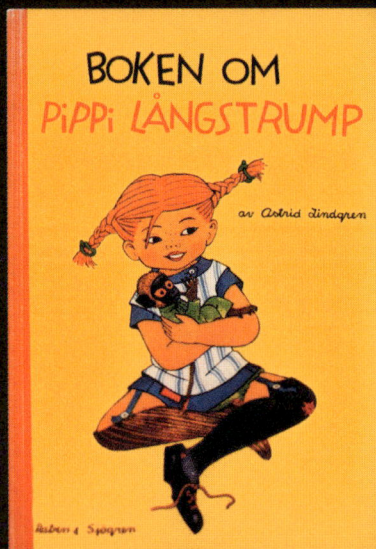

↑ Cover of the Swedish children's
book *Pippi Longstocking* (1945)

宮崎 駿 監督作品

魔女の宅急便

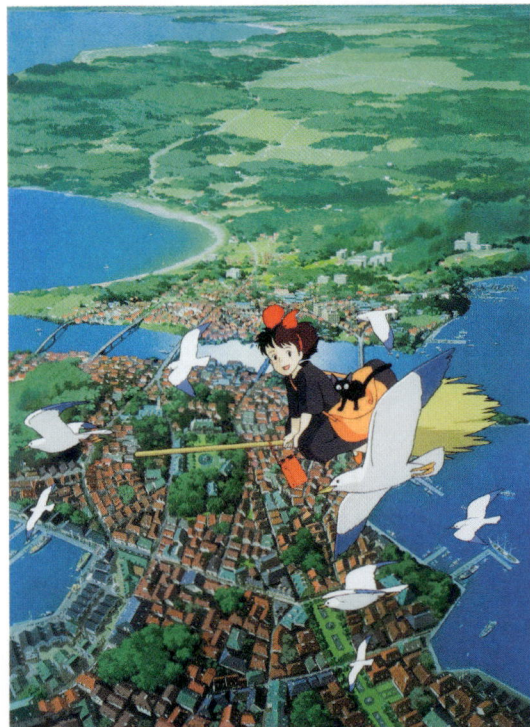

おちこんだりもしたけれど、私はげんきです。

↑ Poster for *Kiki's Delivery Service*,
whose titular heroine encompasses
the spirits of Heidi and Pippi

⬆ Maienfeld, Switzerland, the setting for
Spyri's *Heidi*, which Miyazaki and
colleagues visited in the 1970s

⬆ Visby, Sweden, a well-preserved
medieval Hanseatic town dating
back to the twelfth century

↥ The heroine and a beloved goat in *Heidi, Girl of the Alps*, a television show Miyazaki worked on

↥ Kiki reconnects with her cat friend Jiji and his new family in *Kiki's Delivery Service*

Heidi's story is at root about securing and expressing independence while still growing up, and a similar struggle plays out for a number of Miyazaki protagonists. Perhaps his 1989 feature, *Kiki's Delivery Service*, plays out this struggle most poignantly and – as Takahata and Miyazaki attempted years earlier in *Heidi* – with emotional realism and details from daily life. Based on Eiko Kadono's episodic 1985 children's novel *Majo no Takkyūbin*, *Kiki's* centres on a 13-year-old witch who is leaving her loving family to make her way in the city. In Miyazaki's hands, this budding broom-flying sorcerer lives in an otherwise firmly recognizable reality of houses and shops and all the mundane accoutrements of non-magical life. When she saves a friend from a zeppelin disaster, the death-defying events take place in a common town square and are narrated in the news-break tones of a radio announcer.

That aerial act of derring-do is absent from the book and not par for the course in Miyazaki's film, which dwells on Kiki's efforts to settle in and make a living for herself. She finds mentors in a baker and an artist in a forest, both women, and eventually has to make do without her trusty black cat, Jiji, who is finding his own independence and a romantic interest. This is all in keeping with Miyazaki's proposal for the film, in which he stated that his teenage witch would not be an automatic star by virtue of her magic, and that her ability to fly wasn't a ticket to freedom, but maybe even unsettling. In a real way, just as Heidi doesn't know if she can endure life under a cruel governess in Frankfurt, so does Kiki wonder if she can truly survive amid strangers in the city.

It's a prime example of Miyazaki blending the kind of struggle for independence that recurs in children's literature and the pressing realities of the country he observed around him in the 1980s. In his eyes, young women in Japan struggled to achieve independence not only economically but on the level of self-realization as well. Kiki's magic, which she at one point feels wavering, stands in for anyone finding their footing and sense of purpose. In the same proposal for *Kiki's Delivery Service* – in which he even mentions a contemporary economic buzzword, *furi arubaita* ('job-hopping part-timers') – Miyazaki presents a typically ambitious goal far beyond whiz-bang storytelling: no less than offering 'solidarity to young viewers who find themselves torn between dependence and independence'.[6]

On the *Heidi* series, Miyazaki's particular duties encompassed the spatial organization of the action on screen and maintaining the consistency of both the animation and the backgrounds. As abstract as that might sound, the result is a palpable physical coherence and variety to the movement of characters that is on display from the opening credits, which very nearly flaunt Heidi's dynamism: hurtling on a swing 'into' the camera, prancing with a goat, floating on a cloud and folk dancing. In *Kiki's Delivery Service*, Miyazaki as director was wholly in command, and the spirit of the animation is clear: a young girl heroine engaging with the world, quite literally making her way through it in new and different ways. In some ways *Spirited Away* continues some themes of *Kiki's*, with echoes of a children's book Miyazaki had thought about adapting in 1980, Sachiko Kashiwaba's *The Village Beyond the Mist*, featuring a young girl who takes a trip alone on a train to a rural village, and confronted by a mysterious house, finds herself working in a shopping district run by the descendants of wizards.

Miyazaki worked on many series and features before directing his own, but he seemed to hold a special place for Heidi even decades later. Besides writing most of the text for a 2005 Heidi exhibit at the Ghibli Museum, he also continued an annual December tradition well after that, placing toy animal goats reminiscent of those in *Heidi* in the Studio Ghibli kitchen window.

Creative Risks

How Antoine
de Saint-Exupéry
Helped Miyazaki
Take Flight

The name of Miyazaki's famed animation house, Studio Ghibli, suggests the fanciful moniker of a character from his movies. In fact, *ghibli* is an Arabic term for a hot wind in the North African desert, but the obscure reference reflects an obsession with flight that's at the heart of the artist's work. The word was also bestowed on an Italian model of aircraft that flew in the Sahara in the late 1930s and early 1940s, the Caproni Ca.309 Ghibli. But more to the point, the Sahara and its desert winds loom large in the life of one of Miyazaki's personal lodestars: Antoine de Saint-Exupéry, the aviator and author of the children's book *The Little Prince* (1943) and memoir *Terre des Hommes* (1939, usually translated as *Wind, Sand and Stars*).

The Little Prince, an international classic, ranks high in Miyazaki's estimation of children's literature, perhaps unsurprisingly. But it was *Terre des Hommes* that Miyazaki read in a Japanese paperback when he was 20 years old, an impressionable moment for the artist as a university student. The book recounts how Saint-Exupéry crashed in the Sahara during a 1935 air race and survived four harrowing days in the desert with his mechanic before a Bedouin man rescued them. Before then, the aviator had already logged years of treacherous runs as a postal pilot. 'We cannot possibly feel the sky as they did,' Miyazaki once wrote of Saint-Exupéry's pioneering mail runs, in a commentary for a Japanese edition of *Terre des Hommes*.[7] For Miyazaki, Saint-Exupéry represented a glorious spirit of abandon and risk, part of a bygone era whose vantage on the world will never quite be recaptured. While clearly taken with the aristocratic French hero, who was said to read and write during his longer flights, Miyazaki did not blindly romanticize the man's death, which occurred during a reconnaissance mission in the South of France for the Allies during the Second World War.

(Missing for decades, the plane's wreckage was only identified in 2004 after debris was discovered in 2000.) Rather, Miyazaki believed that Saint-Exupéry's experiences in the sky must have felt humbling, and he recognized how inextricable the beauty of those experiences were from the brutality inherent to these earlier years of aviation technology and to these routine yet risky postal runs.

Miyazaki would tackle the troubling dualism of technology, so often twinned with destruction, late in his career with *The Wind Rises*, based on the life of Jiro Horikoshi, the Japanese engineer who designed the Zero fighter plane. But in 1992, his *Porco Rosso* portrayed the life of an aviator whose very conception seems to dare the viewer to laugh even as it garners respect: a 1930s-era flying ace who's part pig, part man. (Miyazaki's plane choices for the film were wonderfully nerdy: Porco flies an apparent doppelgänger of the Macchi M.33, which competed in the actual 1925 edition of the Schneider Trophy, a seaplane race.)

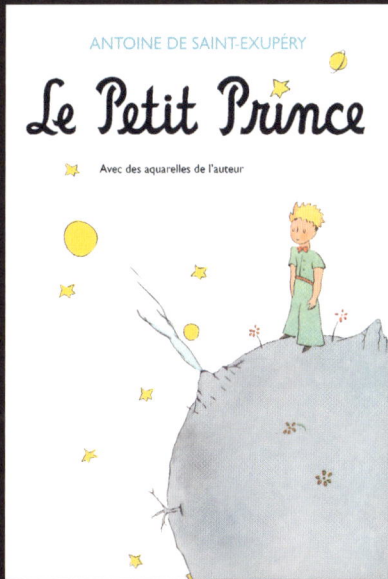

↥ Cover of a 1999 edition of *The Little Prince*
by Antoine de Saint-Exupéry

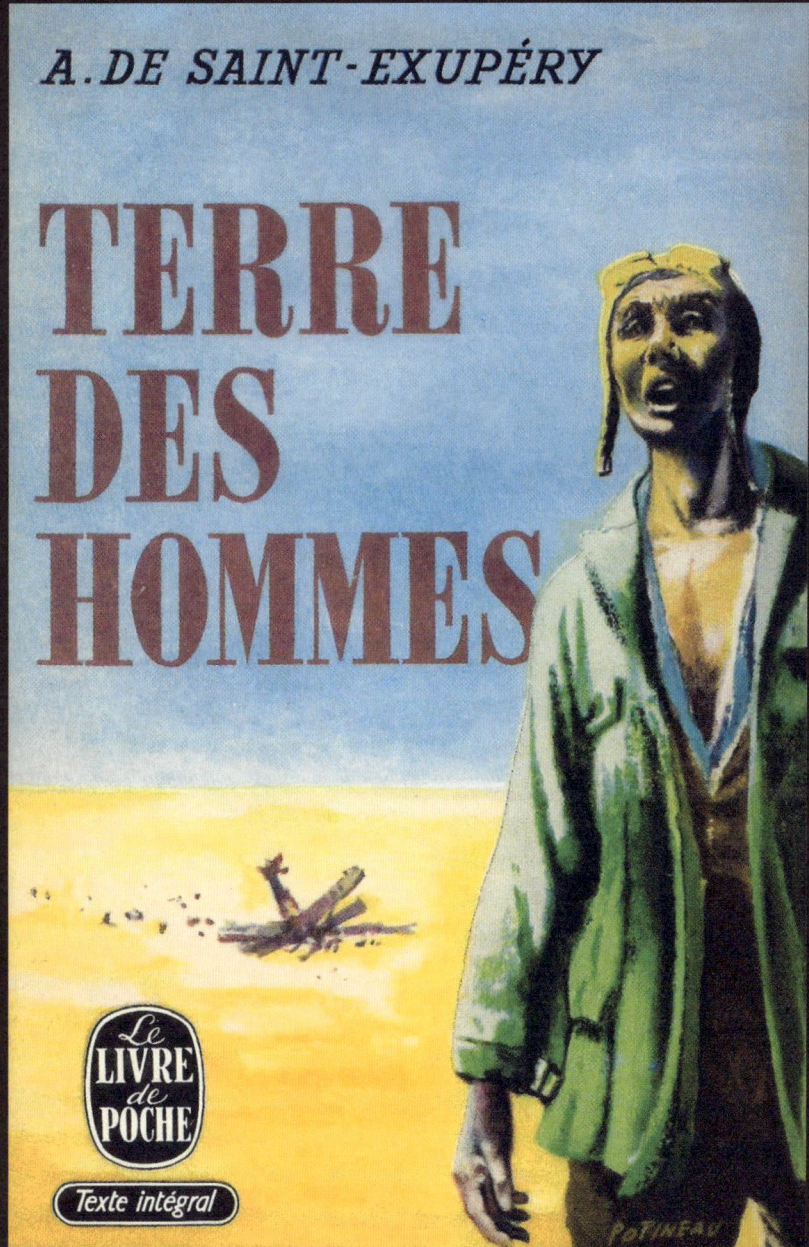

ANTOINE DE SAINT-EXUPÉRY

Le Petit Prince

Avec des aquarelles de l'auteur

A. DE SAINT-EXUPÉRY

TERRE
DES
HOMMES

Le
LIVRE
de
POCHE

Texte intégral

↥ Cover of a 1963 edition of *Terre des Hommes*,
a memoir in the form of autobiographical
essays by Saint-Exupéry

↑ The porcine pilot takes to
the skies in *Porco Rosso*

↑ A Lockheed F-5A Lightning, similar to
the plane Saint-Exupéry was flying when
he crashed off the coast of France

↑ Saint-Exupéry in a plane cockpit,
where he liked to read and write

Living in self-imposed exile in a Mediterranean island cove, Porco has a roughly gallant air to him, maybe like Humphrey Bogart in *Casablanca* (1942), and a chanteuse at an island club, Madame Gina, carries a torch for him. Yet in his original proposal for the film, Miyazaki played up its gently goofy appeal as 'a cartoon movie for tired, middle-aged men whose brain cells have turned to tofu'.[8]

Perhaps Miyazaki was being playful because he did not wish to be seen as attempting to channel his hero Saint-Exupéry, whom he regarded as a genius. But Porco Rosso's dedication to his profession and repeated willingness to risk his life for others are portrayed with an emotional realism quite apart from the story's requisite pirates and fanciful flying machines. His curious state of being – a partial transformation isn't explicitly explained and might even be a kind of self-imposed curse – dramatically expresses his withdrawal from a world which has disillusioned him, and which remains prone to militarization and air conflict even during the film's interwar setting. Only the gumption and innocence of a devoted teenage engineer, Fio, who revamps and maintains his plane, places him back on course.

Miyazaki's casting of the youthful and fearless Fio as a revivifying and inspiring force feels related in spirit to Miyazaki's appreciation of Saint-Exupéry. In *The Little Prince* a pilot who crashes in the Sahara (as the author did) meets an otherworldly boy who suddenly appears and asks the pilot to draw a sheep. They strike up a bond as the boy critiques his next several attempts at drawing – a premise that must have amused Miyazaki – and then recounts stories of planets he has visited. Each planet hosts a single inhabitant who is blinkered by his worldview: a self-absorbed king, a self-pitying drinker, a number-crunching businessman who sees the universe solely in terms of ownership. The pilot and the boy share a scepticism about these reductive viewpoints; each provides solace to the other.

Saint-Exupéry resonates with Miyazaki not only because of his spectacular aerial experiences and implicit courage, but also because of this inner youthful energy that helps make that adult possible. It's a deeply held respect for children's quiddity and immeasurable value that Miyazaki shared with his longtime co-conspirator, Isao Takahata. When the two had attempted to adapt *Pippi Longstocking*, it was precisely the protagonist's audacity that so attracted Takahata, who considered the book 'a bomb that freed children's minds to be just as they were'.[9] The potential of children is something Miyazaki associated quite clearly with Saint-Exupéry's slender but devastating *Little Prince*, as he later recounted when he visited the Sahara himself.

In the spring of 1998, Miyazaki flew from Toulouse to Cape Juby in the Western Sahara in a bright red Antonov biplane, the same model as Saint-Exupéry had, just after releasing *Princess Mononoke* (and announcing his early retirement). The flight itself was transcendent for Miyazaki, who even stuck his arm out at one point to feel the air. But just as emotional was his visit to the airstrip that Saint-Exupéry had managed in the Sahara, which triggered an overwhelming memory from the pilot's writings in *Wind, Sand and Stars*. It's a jarring passage about, as Miyazaki put it, 'the murdering of the Mozart in children . . . resulting in the loss of the supreme possibilities they were born with'. Miyazaki remembers when he was young, resolving to stand with this 'murdered' part of children, and he carried this spirit of celebration of youthful potential throughout his work.[10]

'Saint-Exupéry was a poet,' Miyazaki concludes in his contemporary account of his tribute flight, comparing him to spiralling Japanese poets like Takuboku Ishikawa and Santōka Taneda. 'A gemstone that refused to be polished', he wrote in his introduction to a collection of Saint-Exupéry's drawings. In that sense, Miyazaki's works take inspiration from Saint-Exupéry's search for a philosophy of life, fire-toughened by the dangerous fatalism of flight and preserving the flame of creative discovery and rejuvenation.

PART
THREE

Superhuman Strengths

How *Ponyo* Replaces the Fairy Tale of Hans Christian Andersen's 'The Little Mermaid'

Porco Rosso remains an indelibly eccentric creation, and the porcine pilot is an outlier even within Miyazaki's gallery of curiosities, as the rare lead character who is an adult. It bears repeating that nothing galvanizes Miyazaki as much as the heedless energy and will of youth, reflected in his choices of protagonists. His view of what follows childhood is unsentimental, to say the least: 'As to what happens to children when they grow up – they become normal, boring adults,' he wrote in an afterword to a collection of his writings and interviews.[11] But whatever his feelings about the reality of Japan's adult ranks, he returned to another aspect of Porco Rosso years later with *Ponyo on the Cliff by the Sea* (2008).

Like *Porco Rosso*'s pilot-with-a-pig's-visage, *Ponyo* centres on a character who is not quite human in form. In fact, she is 'a fish with a human face', as Miyazaki simply and gleefully put it when he presented the film's premise to two lead animators at Studio Ghibli.[12] Over the course of the movie, Ponyo yearns to transform completely into a little girl as she grows closer to a friendly five-year-old boy named Sosuke. She is another of Miyazaki's transformed protagonists, like Porco Rosso, or Sophie in *Howl's Moving Castle*, a teenage hatter whom a witch changes into an elderly woman. But as with Saint-Exupéry's heroic significance for Miyazaki, little Ponyo looms large as an emotionally realistic avatar of an unbridled life-force that the animator clearly marvels at, respects and wishes to preserve.

Miyazaki's touchstone for *Ponyo* was Hans Christian Andersen's 'The Little Mermaid', which was published in 1837. The Danish author's fairy tale is a romantic mix of rapturous and visceral. After saving a drowning prince and falling in love with him, a mermaid takes a witch's potion to grow human legs and join him, but at the horrible cost of never returning to her family in the sea and losing her tongue. The prince welcomes the mermaid into his castle but marries someone else who reminds him of her; the mermaid tries to kill herself and ends up ascending to the skies and joining 'the children of the air', who look in on good and wicked boys and girls.

Andersen's story is worth recounting because of how Miyazaki reshapes it into something expressing his worldview, which recentres on identity in an entirely different way. To begin with, Ponyo is the equivalent of a strong-willed kindergartener when we meet her in a swarm of her sister fish, not the marriageable 15-year-old sea maiden (*Meerjungfrau*) that Andersen envisioned. Ponyo's initial metamorphosis transpires not as a result of a witch's bargain, but after an accident, when Sosuke has a cut and she tastes the blood. The potentially macabre detail has echoes in the witch's potion preparations in the Andersen tale, but here it's a gesture born from Ponyo's avid, innocent nature.

↥　The sea maiden among the ornate
　creatures of the deep in Edmund Dulac's
　1911 illustration of 'The Little Mermaid'

⇧   Granmamare, Ponyo's mother, is a wholesale
reimagining of what makes a heroine

⇧   Ponyo, never to be underestimated,
and her thousands of siblings

Ponyo and her adventures proceed with a truly unbounded spirit, in contrast to Andersen's drumbeat of self-sacrifice, which sears away more and more of the mermaid's identity. Miyazaki has an entirely different ideal in mind for his pocket-sized heroine, evidently fond but subject to his own preconceptions: 'Ponyo is the pure manifestation of the feminine principle. She resists all things that restrain her, acts with no thought of consequences and charges ahead to get what she wants. She has no doubts or concerns about eating, hugging or chasing,' he wrote in a 2007 memo to the film's composer Joe Hisaishi. Sosuke, too, gets his own makeover from the oblivious prince: Miyazaki sees the boy as 'brilliant' precisely because 'he accepts all of Ponyo'.

Ponyo therefore becomes another female Miyazaki protagonist whose salient feature is her successful pursuit of freedom. That's not the only way in which Miyazaki creatively departs from Andersen's picture of femininity. The sea witch in 'The Little Mermaid' is a gruesome figure, attended by assorted slithery creatures who ensnare hapless sailors. But Miyazaki instead gives us Ponyo's mother, Granmamare, a powerful life-giving maternal figure who also demonstrates absolute independence in living and ruling apart from Ponyo's saturnine father, Fujimoto, whose literary origins might lie in Andersen's Sea King, the mermaid's father. Granmamare joins Miyazaki's long line of formidable and fascinating matriarchal masterminds, like Dola, the pirate leader in *Laputa: Castle in the Sky*, or the morally complex Lady Eboshi of *Princess Mononoke*.

Although Miyazaki discards the harsh, firmly pre-modern lesson of 'The Little Mermaid', it's possible to see that its fanciful backdrop still enchanted him. Andersen's undersea wonderland is teeming with creatures, both normal and nefarious, and the mermaid and her sisters tend a variety of gardens, including her own with a statue of a human boy. To an animator known for explosions of colourful activity, Andersen's descriptions must have set off sparks in his mind: radiant blue waters, blossoms like flames of fire, a sea palace adorned with deep green and red shells. Andersen's comparison of tumultuous waves to mountains presages Miyazaki's full-screen shots of rolling whitecaps.

Ponyo does make her own consequential sacrifice, joining Sosuke and giving up her magical world to join humans on land for good. It's a happier ending of a sort – she also gains a voice, rather than losing one – but not an uncomplicated one, because her story also unleashes forces beyond her control which threaten the earth with destruction. Miyazaki avoids composing a fairy tale with either a harsh lesson or an easily digestible solution. It's another example of his approach to influences not simply through imitation, amalgam or homage, but by elaborating upon them with transformations and counternarratives – until the fiction becomes wholly his own.

Andersen's mermaid makes her deal with the witch partly in order to gain a soul, which mermaids do not have in Andersen's universe. From Miyazaki's first frames of Ponyo, however, it's clear that she, and the movie, will have a soul and a life of their own from the start.

⬆ Hans Christian Andersen, author of *The Little Mermaid and Other Fairy Tales*, photographed in 1869

Philosophical Fiction

How Do You Live? and
Other Reflections from
Japanese Literature

When Miyazaki was in the planning stages for *Ponyo*, he borrowed a friend's house by the sea to hunker down alone. Pottering about and savouring his solitude, he listened to classical music and read works by Natsume Sōseki, a Japanese writer from the early twentieth century who is also a favourite of Haruki Murakami. Sōseki's most famous books include *I Am a Cat* (1905) and *Kokoro* (1914), and his scepticism towards modernization intrigued Miyazaki, who balances his avowed fondness for intricate flying machines with a devotion to preserving nature in its own complexity. Ponyo's pal, Sosuke, shares his name with a character in Sōseki's 1910 novel *The Gate*, which Miyazaki's magpie tendencies suggest is not a coincidence.

But when Miyazaki was once asked by a publisher to select 50 of his favourite books from children's literature, it might have surprised some fans to find that the overwhelming majority hailed from Western literature: British especially, American, French and Polish too, but only a handful of Japanese stories. Curiously, one such story he named was 'The Restaurant of Many Orders' (1924) by Kenji Miyazawa – in which two travellers in Western dress enter a restaurant and soon realize that they will be eaten as the main course. Miyazaki has even quipped that 'juvenile literature in Japan is still in the minor leagues'[13] during an interview extolling the British author Robert Westall for his bravery in confronting hard truths.

This is of course a playful exaggeration, and for immediate proof one need look no further than Eiko Kadono's *Majo no Takkyūbin*, which Miyazaki mined for *Kiki's Delivery Service*, and which Kadono followed with several sequels. Miyazaki might have been drawn to Kadono partly on the basis of shared personal history: the writer was only five years old when her mother died, creating an absence that resonates with Miyazaki's own experience of loss when his mother fell sick. And as it happens, a drawing had been Kadono's original inspiration for her book: her own 12-year-old daughter's sketch of a witch flying through the sky, listening to the radio.

As in Miyazaki's film, Kadono's Kiki is distinguished not especially by her magic – she flies primarily to ferry goods between people, not to conduct air battles – but by her character. She's determined in the face of obstacles, and she demonstrates a goodness that feels down-to-earth rather than heroic; though she can take flight, she's often weighed down by her doubts. Miyazaki's inspiration centred more on the potential of Kadono's Kiki for deeper characterization than on any particular rambunctious escapades (which the filmmaker had shown himself more than capable of concocting). Other Japanese figures in children's literature that Miyazaki has talked of as inspirations are author Rieko Nakagawa, whose stories were adapted into the Ghibli Museum shorts *Treasure Hunting* and *The Whale Hunt*, and Momoko Ishii, an author and translator who edited the Iwanami children's books series that brought so many Western works to Japan.

↑ Novelist Natsume Sōseki, author
of *I Am a Cat* and *Kokoro*, and
touchstone for Miyazaki

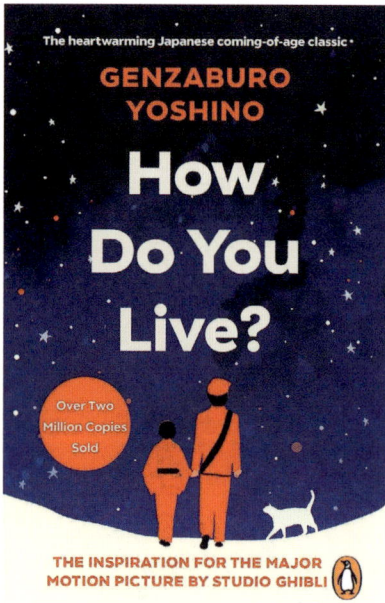

↥ Cover of *How Do You Live?*
by Genzaburō Yoshino

↥ Eiko Kadono, the children's literature
author who wrote the book that inspired
Kiki's Delivery Service

But the Japanese novel that inspired Miyazaki even more deeply was a work that he adapted in name only. His 2023 feature, released in English-language markets as *The Boy and the Heron*, is originally titled *How Do You Live?* – a title taken from Genzaburō Yoshino's 1937 classic. The film tells the tale of a newcomer to the country and the fantastical world he's drawn into by way of a Western-style tower (itself probably a reference to Edogawa Ranpo's mystery novel *Ghost Tower*, for which Miyazaki drew cover art for a new edition). But *How Do You Live?* (the book) might be described as a kind of philosophical fiction aimed at enlightening children. Centring on a 15-year-old boy named Junichi and his friends, it alternates a narrative of Junichi's life as a bright schoolboy and son of a widow, with diary entries by his caring uncle, who ranges far and wide in history and science for illustrative examples.

Junichi's uncle nicknames him Koperu, short for Copernicus. The reference to the astronomer who postulated that the Earth and all other planets orbit the sun, rather than the Earth being the centre of the galaxy, underlines a Miyazakian theme of developing one's true place and perspective in the world. That indeed was the explicit purpose of the book, published by Iwanami Shoten as the climactic entry in its Nihon Shosan Bunko series, or 'The Japan Young People's Library'. Originally intended as a textbook of ethics and the humanities, the book was ultimately written as a novel in an attempt to evade the scrutiny of the militarizing government's special police, who were on the lookout for anti-authoritarian sentiments. Yoshino had previously been jailed for 18 months for his sympathies to socialist thought, and his advice about facing up to bullies or mob rule would have been suspect.

Published in 1937, the book was removed from circulation by 1942, and only returned to print after the war in a bowdlerized edition that shied away from critiques of capitalism or class. Miyazaki first read an excerpt from the book in a textbook in elementary school, but later kept marvelling at Yoshino's bravery in writing an essentially subversive text in the same year that war resurged between Japan and China. In a 2006 essay about *How Do You Live?* for Studio Ghibli's house publication, *Neppu*, the filmmaker remembers encountering the volume as a youth at a used bookstore near his family's home in Tokyo, where they had returned after taking refuge in the countryside during wartime. He writes vividly of turning the book's pages and being moved by an illustration of Koperu in a car riding home through the rain (an illustration of which seems to appear in *The Boy and the Heron*).

Looking back, Miyazaki singled out one passage to explain how Yoshino embeds a vision of a liveable future at a time when Japan was about to undergo vast change with the rise of radical, militaristic nationalism. Typically enough, the filmmaker undertakes a kind of visual forensics. In a scene where Koperu gazes at the city from a department store rooftop, Miyazaki realizes it's a view that soon would be unavailable because of military regulations. Preserving an ordinary vantage point from an earlier era that had vanished, Yoshino reminded his readers (in 1937) that another view of the world had once been possible. It's a subtle note, but Miyazaki took it to heart when reconsidering the book in his 2006 essay: 'The conditions we face in our lives today are not so different from those people faced when Yoshino wrote his book.'[14] *The Boy and the Heron* did not turn out to be an adaptation of *How Do You Live?* (though the book does make an appearance). But in some sense, all Miyazaki films might be considered adaptations of the book, as their protagonists seek and find their own answers to Yoshino's eternal question. As Miyazaki put it in his essay, and as he embodied in the people and landscapes he creates in his films, heroism might just be a matter of learning how 'to keep living without giving up our humanity'.

↑ Mahito and Lady Himi outside the magically secluded
birthing chamber where they find his missing stepmother,
Natsuko, who is Himi's sister, in *The Boy and the Heron*

CHAPTER THREE

ALL
THE
WORLD'S
A
STAGE

The Actual Places That Inspire
Miyazaki's Realistic Fantasies

The Bathhouse of *Spirited Away*

How to Build an Enchanting Spot

For all the literary echoes in the worlds of Miyazaki, his films also borrow elements from real-life locations on Earth. It's precisely that fusion of fantasy and fact which makes his films take root in the imagination of viewers and acquire a life all of their own. Magical phenomena may happen, characters may fly through the air, but Miyazaki has no interest in pure escapism. The sea kingdom in *Ponyo*, for example, was conceived as 'the underworld next door', as Miyazaki put it in his memo to composer Joe Hisaishi – a neat way of expressing fully fleshed-out worlds where we can still get lost. The touches of reality somehow make the flights of fancy even more intense.

Spirited Away is one of the most phantasmagorical works Miyazaki has ever created. One Japanese tagline for the movie promised a trip to a *fushigi* village, deploying the same word used to translate 'Wonderland' in Japanese editions of *Alice's Adventures in Wonderland*. Ten-year-old Chihiro follows her parents through a tunnel that leads to a deserted row of buildings and a towering bathhouse, which is where Miyazaki fully unleashes the film's unruly magic. But before they reach these buildings, the movie reproduces specific markers of contemporary Japan: Chihiro mopes in the back seat of the family's Audi as her father drives up to housing developments. Getting this kind of banal but true-to-life detail right (even including telephone poles in roadside scenery) is a priority for Miyazaki: in the documentary *10 Years with Hayao Miyazaki* (2019), he installs a camera in his car to record all the forgettable ordinary details he passes in driveways through the neighbourhood.

Miyazaki's attention to realistic detail continues when Chihiro and her parents broach an entirely alternate realm on the other side of the tunnel. After passing a clock tower in a field, they walk along two-storey structures that have colourful, curving facades and arcade-style entrances, facing on a dirt street strung with red lanterns. The model for these buildings is the Edo-Tokyo Architectural Museum, an open-air collection of 30-odd structures from nineteenth- and early twentieth-century Tokyo that were preserved and relocated there. A favourite spot for Miyazaki to visit, it's where he made an official public announcement about *Spirited Away*, and its restored buildings were studied by the production team. (He even designed the museum's mascot, Edomaru, a green caterpillar.) The open-air museum is distinguished by the 'billboard architecture' (*kanban kenchiku*) of the buildings; in *Spirited Away*, one building is decorated with celestial motifs, a shooting star and a crescent moon.

In the empty streets, the festive variety of the prewar buildings already gives off a slightly eerie, possibly enchanted quality. Chihiro's mother notices that, strangely, all the shopfronts are restaurants (which Miyazaki supposedly modelled on entertainment districts). Following the tantalizing smell of food being cooked, Chihiro's mother and father sit down at one open counter where stacks of chicken, dumplings, sausages and other food-stall goodies are piled high. They gorge themselves, and when Chihiro returns from wandering, she finds they have transformed into pigs. The gluttony-related metamorphosis feels like something out of a fairy tale, and echoes the Kenji Miyazawa story Miyazaki is fond of, 'The Restaurant of Many Orders' (1924), about an unattended eatery that turns out to be a trap, and a folktale parable about greed called 'Home of the Sparrow'.

↥ Edo-Tokyo Open-Air Architectural Museum, which preserves buildings from the past, informs Miyazaki's conception of the village in *Spirited Away*

↥ Chihiro wanders an enchanted village before discovering the bathhouse in *Spirited Away*

The sequence is just Miyazaki's appetizer. Up some stairs and across a bridge lies the centrepiece of the film and its action: a towering bathhouse that shares its self-contained plenitude with the castles and islands from other Miyazaki films. Snuck in by a protective young man named Haku, Chihiro finds a bustling world of bath workers and the multiform spirits and gods who are their guests. As with many Miyazaki creations, it's tough to pin down any single influence for the bathhouse, which melds both Eastern and Western influences with its paper walls and elevators. Miyazaki's concept of a resort for spirits grew out of his fascination with the Shimotsuki festival in Nagano Prefecture, a ritual in which masked villagers invite gods to bathe. But two other possible reference points are the Nikkō Tōshogū shrine, with its ornate top-heavy facade, and the Dogo Onsen, a three-thousand-year-old hot spring located on the island of Shikoku and often described as the oldest in Japan. Dogo Onsen was a familiar place to Studio Ghibli staff, as it was the site of a company vacation. (While readily identifiable to a Japanese viewer, the building was glossed in the American release with an added dubbed line: 'It's a bathhouse.')

54

↪
The exterior of Dogo Onsen, one of the oldest such bathhouses, in Matsuyama, Japan

↑ Chihiro and her parents, who are turned
into pigs after eating in the enchanted
village in *Spirited Away*

↥ The Meguro Gajoen, a historic hotel and wedding venue in Tokyo that was one of the inspirations for *Spirited Away*

↥ The bustling bathhouse glitters at night in *Spirited Away*

The multilevel bathhouse with its ornate decorations and amenities was also inspired by the Meguro Gajoen in Tokyo, originally built in 1931 as an all-in-one wedding and banquet complex. Inside the film's bathhouse, dubbed Arubaya, individual floors and areas draw on assorted sources. The boiler room, where the spider-like caretaker Kamaji keeps the furnace running, has walls full of small drawers modelled on a 1927 stationery shop. Flower patterns and sliding doors in the building were drawn from paintings in Kyoto's Nijō Castle, residence of a famous shogun. The bathhouse's employee dorms, where Chihiro stays, above the boiler room, evoke quarters for the women who worked in textile companies, according to Miyazaki. And at the top of the building, where Yubaba the executive and enchantress lives, the opulent decor evokes the Rokumeikan, a Meiji-era restaurant and guesthouse used to welcome Western diplomats.

The pastiche in the *Spirited Away* bathhouse shows Miyazaki's modus operandi of plucking styles and details from the world at large and populating the structure with his imagination. His producer, Toshio Suzuki, when called upon to write an introduction for a monograph by the museum of the Academy of Motion Picture Arts and Sciences, dwells precisely on these vast reserves of his partner's 'visual memory'. But the air of fantasy is never far: later in the film, Chihiro takes an eerily serene train away from the bathhouse that was explicitly inspired from yet another Miyazawa story, *Night on the Galactic Railroad*. Reality and fantasy are never far apart, and maybe never even separate categories, in the work of Miyazaki.

Into the Woods

Yakushima Island,
Sayama Hills
and the Foresting
of *Princess Mononoke*
and *My Neighbor Totoro*

Off the coast of Kyushu, Japan's southernmost main island, is Yakushima, home to Japanese cedars that can be over a thousand years old. The tree canopy enhances the momentous hush of the forest, which feels all the more secluded on an island. It was here that the Studio Ghibli team went on a scouting trip in April 1995 in preparation for creating *Princess Mononoke*, the period epic centred on a majestic forest, the creatures and spirits that live there, and the people who threaten its existence. It was, for Miyazaki, a return: years earlier, he had made a pilgrimage to Yakushima to visit the Jōmon-sugi, a tree believed to be over seven millennia old.

Princess Mononoke is partly built around the aesthetics of this forest. The distinctive visual patterns and rhythms in nature have echoes in the film's backgrounds and even its action. Mossy green colours and dappled light are faithfully rendered, as are the rippling trunks and roots of old-growth forests; one tree covered with drops of water – seen when the young warrior who is the protagonist, Ashitaka, awakens from a sleep – was a tree encountered on the scouting trip. Miyazaki also repeatedly creates a through-line viewpoint familiar to many hikers: peering through trees and seeing a figure hove into view, perhaps into a shaft of light (another favourite Miyazaki motif), as when the forest spirit silently appears in the film.

Yakushima's mountainous topography might have inspired the rocky slopes that the wolf goddess Moro or Ashitaka's elk race and leap up and down, a kind of terrain that Miyazaki often favours for his animation, perhaps because of the potential for movement and backgrounds. Even Miyazaki's assignment for the background designer of forest scenes is tailor-made to Yakushima: the animator hails from Kyushu, and the beauty he portrayed is a purposeful counterpoint to the bloodshed in the film.

Yet curiously, when asked about the source for the forest in *Princess Mononoke*, Miyazaki generalized. 'It is a depiction of the forest that has existed within the hearts of Japanese from ancient times,' he told one questioner in 1998 at the Berlin Film Festival, where the movie screened out of competition. Though it might sound like a sidestep, his comment speaks to the transcendent importance of the forest, and nature generally to Miyazaki. In animating the settings of *Princess Mononoke*, he is no longer simply seeking to get the details right for an actual geographic place, but is projecting how the world looked like in even wilder, more uncultivated eras – a preoccupation of Miyazaki, an eager amateur historian of Japan. Nature in its primeval state, wherever it occurs in Japan, holds a nearly spiritual appeal for Miyazaki, as a place of purity where he can return and recharge; he effectively creates these kind of primeval states on screen where stories can grow.

↦
Yakushima Island in Kagoshima Prefecture, Japan, known for its verdant cedar forests and wildlife, was visited by the Studio Ghibli team

←
Mononoke rides
wolf goddess Moro,
surrounded by the
kodama forest spirits

When we say *Princess Mononoke* is inspired by Yakushima Island, then, it is not as a postcard-perfect preserve, but as a living, wild place. The violence and turmoil that runs throughout the movie – battles between spirits and humans, animal figures like Moro that feel palpably, teeth-baringly wild – reflect Miyazaki's firmly held belief that depictions of nature should reflect what he calls 'the irrationality, cruelty and brutality of life itself'.[15] It's an ethos that bursts forth most apparently and radically in *Princess Mononoke*, which stages a battle between human tribes over how to exploit the forest, though it also underpins the futuristic landscapes of *Nausicaä of the Valley of the Wind* and the oceanic upheaval in *Ponyo*.

Throughout, Miyazaki's portrayals of nature can be described as part of his counter-anthropocentric worldview. 'Our way of thinking is that nature exists and human beings exist within it,' he said of Studio Ghibli's philosophy at the 1998 Berlin Film Festival. Plants, weather, time's passage in nature, rays of sunlight and wind are all part of the landscape. In turn, humans are simply one component of the same. This notion of existing within the context of nature is a sensation that also comes through, in a different way, in *My Neighbor Totoro*, which, like *Princess Mononoke*, draws on actual locales while also expressing general truths.

↑ Sayama Hills, a real-life analogue to Totoro's forest

↑ A tree with *shimenawa*, a sacred rope, which can also be seen on the camphor tree in *My Neighbor Totoro*

The influence of Sayama Hills on Totoro's famed world is no secret. It has attracted tourism and even an environmental initiative called 'Totoro's Forest', a nature preserve formed from land purchased through donations (with Miyazaki's providing one of five inaugural contributions). Set in the 1950s, *My Neighbor Totoro* portrays a mix of farmland, wetlands and forest in Tokorozawa, less than 50 kilometres (31 miles) from the Tokyo metropolitan area. (The particular border zone between farmland and hills is known as *satoyama*.) This isn't the stand-alone natural fortress of Yakushima Island but rather a 3,500-hectare (8,650-acre) refuge amid a greater suburban sprawl, no less thriving with wildlife thanks to hundreds of species of plants and animals.

In *My Neighbor Totoro*, Satsuki and Mei and their father are fresh arrivals to the area, and we see their new surroundings with the enthusiastic attention of children exploring a new home. Bugs, tiny leaves, flowers and acorns strewn about are all objects of fascination, as the two sisters race around and laugh and chatter over their discoveries. Their father already acts as if he feels at home (and, as some sharp-eyed fans have pointed out, studies books about trees), and so it is the children who embody the family's integration into their natural surroundings. Miyazaki takes care to reference a sense of the exotic or escapist by fleshing out characters who are already comfortable in this environment, such as the older woman who looks after them and a farm boy who brings a welcome basket and regards the peppy sisters with wide eyes.

Totoro's own home is a kind of tree that can be found in Sayama Hills: a camphor, which is where Mei finds him snoozing, framed by ferns and yellow and pink blossoms. Besides providing a cosy hollow for this snoring creature, the camphor also has religious connotations as a home for protective spirits. Miyazaki decorates the tree in the film with a sacred rope (*shimenawa*) festooned with jagged paper pendants. It's the film's serene centre (albeit with a sometimes mischievous inhabitant) and one that tunes into the possibilities for integrating with nature, rather than bending it to one's will. As *Princess Mononoke* shows, that equilibrium is constantly shifting throughout the work of an artist who knows that he, too, cannot bend nature's energies to the simple purposes of a message or a moral: he can but convey its strength and beauty.

↑ Poster for *My Neighbor Totoro*, showing
Totoro and the sisters Satsuki and Mei
on the camphor tree

Dreaming Up Europe

How Porco Rosso
and Lupin Drift
Across a Continent

Years before Studio Ghibli, the first feature that Miyazaki directed was a careening 1979 caper, *Lupin III: The Castle of Cagliostro*, about a master thief. It's perhaps less known to fans who associate him with his movies from the 1980s and onwards, but Miyazaki's debut was the second feature adaptation from a popular Japanese manga series, which had previously been developed into a TV series Miyazaki had toiled on. But the original Arsène Lupin was a gentleman criminal created by French writer Maurice Leblanc in 1905. And in keeping with the character's European origins, Miyazaki's Lupin drives a Fiat 500, first seen laden with loot from the Monte Carlo Casino and racing through twisting hillside roads. He schemes to infiltrate the villainous Count Cagliostro's castle, a Franco–Czech–Germanic blend of fairy-tale turrets and roofs. The castle's centrepiece is a clock tower that serves a pivotal, deadly purpose in the film's climax, a super-sized version of the sort seen in European town squares.

The Duchy of Cagliostro might reasonably be compared to the actual city state of Monaco, but it's also simply a concocted locale, a Monaco of the mind, as the hybrid-design castle suggests. Indeed, an ideal of Europe had loomed in Miyazaki's imagination long before he travelled there to scout with Isao Takahata for the *Heidi* series earlier in the 1970s. Remembering another scouting trip to Stockholm for the failed *Pippi Longstocking* adaptation, he said: 'Before I went there, I honestly thought I could depict Europe without ever having to see it.'[16]

On that particular trip, Miyazaki forayed out of his cosy hotel and its scheduled meals to visit Skansen, an open-air museum (shades of the one that inspired *Spirited Away*). His urge to be meticulous about Europe's sights ultimately ran into his usual imaginative drive to synthesize and expand upon what he sees, resulting in an intensified amalgam that feels hard to pin down to a specific place.

In his career to that point, Monaco was only the latest European location he had helped bring to screen, following *Little Norse Prince Valiant* (aka *Hols: Prince of the Sun*), *Heidi*, *Dog of Flanders*, *Anne of Green Gables* and *From the Apennines to the Andes* (for which Miyazaki again scouted locations, in Italy and Argentina). For *Porco Rosso*, he returned to exploring the iconography of the Mediterranean, providing locations for its acts of aerial derring-do (and lazing about) on either coast of the Adriatic Sea, Italian and Croatian. Miyazaki's film expands upon his 15-page watercolour manga *The Age of the Flying Boat* from 1989–90 about one Porco Rosso, aka Lieutenant Marco Pagotto. Formerly a pilot of the Italian Navy, Porco is a bounty hunter of the air pirates that are a scourge in the cash-strapped late 1920s setting (and according to the manga, originally a native of Geneva, oddly enough). *The Age of the Flying Boat* names the geographical locations in the area – Lake Maggiore, Milano, the Tyrrhenian Sea, the Istrian Peninsula – that will appear in some form in *Porco Rosso*.

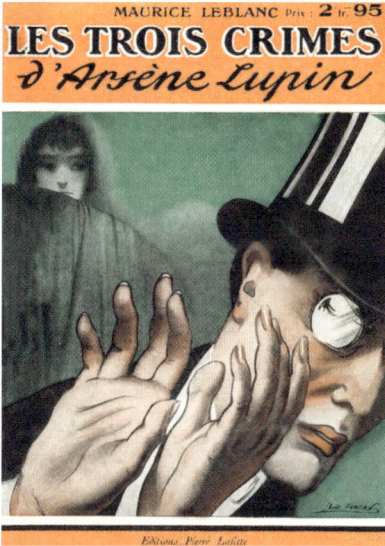

↑ Cover of *Les Trois Crimes d'Arsène Lupin* by Maurice Leblanc

↑ Lupin races his Fiat 500 along winding roads in *Lupin III: The Castle of Cagliostro*

↑ The Stelvio Pass between Italy and Switzerland, a curvy road that evokes the chases of *Lupin III: The Castle of Cagliostro*

↑ Borromeo Palace on Isola Bella in
Lake Maggiore, one possible model
for Hotel Adriano in *Porco Rosso*

↑ Porco Rosso and American aviator
Donald Curtis, recruited by pirates
to defeat the porcine pilot

Porco Rosso has largely withdrawn from society to live in a secret cove accessible only by plane. Croatians have been proud to identify his refuge as the island of Vis, which harbours a beach inlet between high cliffs that is known as Stiniva. Miyazaki soon sends Porco Rosso off to a couple of town locations when his plane requires upkeep of one kind or another. To pay off the loan on the plane, the pilot visits the city of Dubrovnik, Croatia, unmistakable as a sunny fortress-on-the-water, with red clay tile roofs and tan limestone walls. Mechanical maintenance necessitates a visit to the other side of the Adriatic Sea, to Milan, Italy, where his aeronautic-genius friend Piccolo runs a workshop (Piccolo S.P.A., Italian for incorporated). Piccolo's women-dominated staff includes his brilliant granddaughter Fio, Porco Rosso's future co-pilot. Miyazaki sets the Piccolo warehouse in an industrial area abutting a waterway, though other glimpses of the city look perhaps less Milanese and more Roman.

One of the film's settings at sea, Hotel Adriano, holds a special romantic significance for Porco Rosso. A favoured haunt of pilots, Hotel Adriano is the island hotel managed by Gina, elegant chanteuse and Porco Rosso's former paramour, who muses whether they might ever be together again. Her cosmopolitan air lends this and other aspects of the film an echo of the classical Hollywood film and repertory staple *Casablanca*, starring Humphrey Bogart (himself, like Porco Rosso, a bit of a *jolie-laide* figure) and Ingrid Bergman. By the time of the film, of course, riffs on *Casablanca* and its fatalist romantic dialogue had become so common in movies and TV shows that *Porco Rosso* is just as much evoking a feeling of nostalgia as the film itself.

↥ Humphrey Bogart poses at the entrance of Rick's Café from *Casablanca* (1942)

Much like Rick's Café in *Casablanca,* Hotel Adriano in *Porco Rosso* offers up an international outpost as the liminal setting for romance and other dreams that might never be realized. The hotel is a quintessential Miyazakian location: a sprawling castle-like complex with a bushy forested garden, all perched on a high-walled island surrounded by azure seas – a place that, overgrown with vines, looks like the physical manifestation of an ideal, or a memory, overtaken by time. While it has been compared to the grand, sprawling Isola Bella in Italy's Lake Maggiore, Hotel Adriano has a visionary purity that's all its own.

Porco Rosso and the goggled, barrel-chested pirates he tangles with are not entirely set apart from the embattled time period of the late 1920s, with Europe on the eve of another world war and frightening aspirations to power. Our porcine hero at one point takes a vocal stand against Fascism, proclaiming 'better a pig than a Fascist', and he faces off against an arrogant American pilot with the jawline of Errol Flynn who aspires to be president someday. Even a light-seeming fantasy hybrid does not escape the ruminations on history percolating through Miyazaki's memory.

A Working Notion

How Wales and Striking Unions Ground *Laputa: Castle in the Sky*

'The setting is vaguely European,' Miyazaki wrote in his production outline for *Laputa: Castle in the Sky*, his 1986 film about a boy-and-girl duo of orphans who fend off airborne pirates and sinister military forces to reach a legendary floating kingdom. In fact, in preproduction, the animator went on a location-scouting trip to specific places: England and Wales, in 1985. The film's hero, Pazu, is introduced toiling in a Welsh mining town, where he meets Sheeta, his orphan counterpart, when she falls out of the sky. That could take anyone by surprise, but her arrival feels especially noteworthy amid the routines followed by Pazu and his fellow miners, focused on the earth rather than the heavens.

Castle in the Sky is set in a fanciful nineteenth century of flying machines and robots, but Miyazaki's trip to Wales took place shortly after very real and tumultuous events in England in 1984. Under the policies of Margaret Thatcher, at least 20 mines and 20,000 coal mining jobs were targeted for termination by the National Coal Board; the National Union of Mineworkers eventually carried out a forceful strike. Miyazaki had come of age in Japan as a student at Gakushuin University amid historic demonstrations: not only the Anpo protests but also labour strikes as workers at the Mitsui Miike Coal Mine in 1960 fought sweeping job cuts. His degree was in political science and economics with a focus on Japanese industrial theory, and he often discussed the Anpo issue, economics and ideology generally with his mother.

Miyazaki went on to become a fierce union activist himself after he was hired by the anime studio Toei Doga, and in 1964 became its union's general secretary. He made fast friends with the vice president, Isao Takahata, his future collaborator and Ghibli co-founder. Decades later, he referenced notions of solidarity in talking about the animation industry. 'If the drawings are mass produced by . . . staff members who have no sense of solidarity or unity to begin with, the life really goes out of them,' he said in a 1988 lecture,[17] not long after co-founding Studio Ghibli, which had released *Castle in the Sky* as its first feature.

On his trip through the Rhondda Valley in south Wales, Miyazaki saw abandoned machinery and mines, visited the Big Pit National Coal Museum that had just been opened to the public and witnessed the aftermath of the punishing strikes and related privation. In the film, Pazu lives in a village dubbed Slag Ravine that has Welsh-adjacent terraced houses and dramatic slopes, where Pazu greets the morning with an anthem on his trumpet, a melody that's now somewhat of a mimetic internet sensation.

The miners whom Pazu supports as a mechanic are moustachioed brawny men in overalls who look like salt-of-the-earth figures as envisioned by an admiring visitor like Miyazaki. When the air pirates threaten the boy, they flex their muscles and rush to his defence. They are, as Miyazaki said in a 2005 interview with the *Guardian*, 'a dying breed of fighting men', whom he admired just as he respected the striking coal miners in Japan. In the background of an interior scene in a house, we can see a poster for a miners' protest. Even Pazu's name harkens back to Miyazaki's student days: it was the name of a sailor character he had come up with then.

↑ British miners march in force in Sunderland, England, during the national miners' strike of 1984

↑ Japanese miners, wearing protective gear, lock arms to block strikebreakers in 1960 at Kumamoto

↑   The Stockholm City Hall clock tower
(106m/348ft tall), echoed by a similar
tower in *Kiki's Delivery Service*

⇡   Powis Castle and Garden, Wales, which
Miyazaki visited in 1984, admiring the
mettle of the country's inhabitants and
the beauty of its landscape

⇡   The miners in Pazu's hometown
stand up for him against the pirates
in *Laputa: Castle in the Sky*

⇡ The old town of Colmar in Alsace, France,
is one of the quintessential European locales
that fed Miyazaki's inspiration

⇡ Sophie rides a tram in the European-esque
lands of *Howl's Moving Castle*

Castle in the Sky, then, is rooted in a deep emotional connection that Miyazaki felt – a sense of solidarity rather than a touristic appropriation of an evocative Welsh landscape. Miyazaki drew from his trip not only for Pazu's village, but also more dreamlike settings: the titular castle in the sky, Laputa, resembles Powis Castle and Garden in Wales – if it was a floating fortress unattached to the rest of the land, that is. (*Flying Treasure Island*, incidentally, was another early title Miyazaki considered for the film, showing his continued fondness for children's literature.)

This was not the end of Miyazaki's Welsh connection, however. In the 2000s, Studio Ghibli would adapt *Howl's Moving Castle* from the book by Diana Wynne Jones; the (vaguely punk-sounding) moniker 'Howl' is an anglicized version of the Welsh masculine name Hywel. As with *Castle in the Sky*, Miyazaki in *Howl's Moving Castle* again focuses on a hard-working protagonist who might otherwise blend into the crowd: a young hatmaker named Sophie. Her life changes wildly twice, when she is transformed into a senior citizen and when she boards the mobile fortress of the dashing wizard named Howl who saves her from leering soldiers early in the film.

But whereas Jones's book takes place in Wales, Miyazaki resituates part of his movie in a locale resembling the Alsace region of France, perhaps because he had already explored the Welsh milieu. The city of Colmar features the same half-timbered houses – where wood beams trace distinctive triangle outlines across plaster or brick walls – as in Miyazaki's *Howl's Moving Castle*: such is the alternating-colour town where Sophie lives, Market Chipping, surrounded by verdant green hills. The houses are not uncommon in other cities across Europe, but as Jones herself put it, Colmar's concentration lends a particular 'fairy tale' aspect.

The moving castle has a magical door that opens on to different locations depending on the setting of a multicolour dial, therefore allowing Miyazaki to reference even more locations (not that he would need an excuse, of course). One of these destinations, and another key setting of the film, is Kingsbury, the royal capital of Ingary. Here the style is neoclassical rather than medieval gothic: stately columned buildings and patrician plazas of the sort that might be found in numerous cities in France (where producer Toshio Suzuki noticed critics were intrigued by the Picasso-like structure of the castle). There's a distinctive contrast between Sophie's artisanal background in Market Chipping and the power centre of Kingsbury, home to the Royal Palace, from which the king rules with the sorceress Suliman.

Howl's dial-a-location castle might be a good metaphor for Miyazaki's own location-hopping, harkening back to *Kiki's Delivery Service*, which also centred on a hard-working young woman. Preparations for that film involved trips to Stockholm and Visby, Sweden; hence details such as a clock tower based on Stockholm City Hall. Yet the fictional city where Kiki establishes herself is more accurately described as a European amalgam than a replica Swedish town. All in one place, Miyazaki blends the cascading quality of houses on a Mediterranean coastal town and trams that might better fit in Lisbon, Portugal. You could call the style 'vaguely European', to quote Miyazaki, or just a working notion of Europe.

CHAPTER FOUR

NATIONAL TREASURES

Homegrown Japanese Influences on Miyazaki,
from the Spiritual to the Culinary

Worlds
Within
Worlds

The Natural Role
of Animism in
Miyazaki's Films

As *Spirited Away* opens, Chihiro and her family are on their way to their new house in a housing development. She clutches a farewell bouquet of flowers, so tightly, in fact, that she crushes them, leading her to complain to her mother that they died. It's not the end of the world, obviously, though it will mean the beginning of a new world for Chihiro, and this being a Miyazaki film, the notion of another realm takes on a special meaning. When her father turns the Audi onto a dirt road into a forest, they pass a pile of hollow stone squares, glimpsed in a quick shot and identified by her mother as objects from a shrine, and a *tori* (shrine) gate leaning against a tree. Then, the car whizzes by an anthropomorphic statue of some sort amid the trees, like a relic of an overgrown kingdom (and vaguely like a *daruma* doll). Finally, her father nearly collides at high speed with a similar stone figure when the road suddenly opens upon a red gatehouse of some sort.

There follows a simple but defining image in a film full of grander, florid imagery: a head-on shot of Chihiro standing side by side with the statue, fidgeting and saying she refuses to walk through the tunnel in the gatehouse. The tableau composition rhymes with an iconic shot in another movie, *My Neighbor Totoro*: Satsuki standing next to Totoro at the bus stop in the rain (and carrying her sister, Mei). In one case we have the unclassifiable Totoro, a being whom Miyazaki has refused to define exactly but is clearly a forest spirit (*kami*) of some kind; in the *Spirited Away* case, Chihiro flanks a *dojoshin*, a Shinto monument that houses a spirit, wards off evil and can mark an area as sacred. Both shots in different ways let us sit with an uncanny moment for a human character who finds herself sharing space – and sharing what she thought was her sole reality – with another being. It's a device to which Miyazaki returns later, at the lavish bathhouse in the world on the other end of the tunnel, when Chihiro rides an elevator next to a walrus-sized 'radish spirit' (*oshira-sama* in the original Japanese, or 'great white lord').

↥ Two examples of a deer mandala from
Japan's Muromachi Period (1392–1573),
which fascinates Miyazaki

↥ The regal Forest Spirit, glimpsed from
a distance, in *Princess Mononoke*

⬆ Spirit guests swathed in robes at
the bathhouse in *Spirited Away*

⬆ A 'radish spirit' (*oshira-sama*) riding the elevator
with Chihiro at the bathhouse in *Spirited Away*

⬆ Totoro and Satsuki (carrying her sister, Mei) at the bus stop in *My Neighbor Totoro*

⬆ Chihiro glowers at her parents while standing next to a Shinto monument outside the entrance to the enchanted world in *Spirited Away*

Shinto belief – to whose pantheon of spirits *oshira-sama* belongs – seems particularly well suited to Miyazaki's creations in all their multiplicity. Its varied and adaptable traditions take for granted that *kami* of all kinds pervade the natural world in its many manifestations. Long pre-dating the arrival of Buddhism in Japan during the sixth century, it's a belief system deeply rooted in Japanese culture, and its view of an interconnectedness between people and the spirit world, and of a kind of purity immanent to nature, dovetails with Miyazaki's films, which bring a complexity and sense of paradox to the encounters between humans and other beings. (*Inari* shrines appear throughout *My Neighbor Totoro*, as do *jizo* statues when Mei gets lost.) While films like *Ponyo* and *Princess Mononoke* offer

nuanced and conflicting views of our relationships with nature, Miyazaki's perspective avoids simply projecting a human sense of autonomy or awareness onto the environment in the manner of much animated art. It's an artistic matter as much as anything: 'The more we humans anthropomorphize something and make it an easy target for empathy, the less interesting it becomes.'[18]

Any attempt to fit the films within a particular spiritual framework therefore runs into Miyazaki's resistance to being pinned down and his intuitive approach to fleshing out his worlds. The cavalcade of spirits in *Spirited Away* does draw on the artist's fascination with the annual Shimotsuki festival in Toyama Valley in Nagano Prefecture, during which spirits are summoned to bathe.

While Miyazaki celebrates animism as a part of Japanese identity, he was reluctant simply to populate *Spirited Away* from the back catalogues of Japanese folklore: 'In principle, I didn't want my designs of Japanese spirits to be based on existing images.'[19] While the towering forest spirit in *Princess Mononoke* is inspired by legends of giant *yōkai* known as *daidoboshi*, the film's multitude of *kodama* homunculi – those curious bobble-heads that make a noise like a rattle – seem to arise more from Miyazaki's general sense of the way a forest has a kind of secret life, sometimes visible, sometimes not. And when it comes to Totoro, he sidesteps comparisons to cuddly *tanuki* (raccoon dogs) with a cheery opaqueness: 'There's no need to understand everything. When I'm asked what a *totoro* is, I don't know myself.'[20]

↑ The Shimotsuki festival to summon spirits and bathe them, a local ritual that piqued Miyazaki's interest

↥ Ashitaka rides forth while fending off
a demon in *Princess Mononoke*

Above all, Miyazaki's spirits do not exist for the benefit of humans, nor do they necessarily even wish to understand us. In *Princess Mononoke*, the demon spirits are actively maleficent in nature, manifest in the horrid worm-like extrusions that bring down Nago the boar god and afflict Ashitaka with a cursed wound that he's told leads to certain death. And even if the universally beloved Totoro welcomes the two children in his tree rituals and summons the Catbus for them, he retains an independence, even aloofness, which skirts the sort of scenes of sympathy with Satsuki that one might expect. He and other spirits seem to be Miyazaki's expression of a fundamental part of Japan that might, in fact, be at risk of being lost or forgotten amid the perpetual churn of urbanization and modernization.

Yet Miyazaki has a sense of humour about the role of animism in this modern world, joking about how the *tenjin* (a *kami* associated with scholarship) has become a routine receptacle for students cramming for exams, or how he avoids worshipping at shrines at the New Year. The panoply of spirits and creatures in his films seem instead a way to reach back to an even more primal sense of the earth and its forests and spirits and humans, perhaps even before names and categories were attached. This isn't a nostalgic urge borne of the belief in some lost paradise of the past far from Audis and housing developments, but rather a call to be in touch with the here and now as it is still available in nature today – or in the parlance of our times, to touch grass a little.

Unnatural
Disasters

How Environmental
History Reverberates in
Miyazaki's Creations

Miyazaki's environmental awareness extends beyond the borders of either his country or the current era. The animator is an avowed admirer of the broadleaf evergreen forest culture, a historical paradigm advanced by ethnobotanist Sasuke Nakao, who wrote about a prehistoric forest spanning much of Asia, including southwest Japan. Nakao described a common culture to this vast expanse, rooted in the forest, and eventually becoming part of the culture of the Jomon Period, during the millennia of the area's Neolithic Period (13,000 to 300 BCE). For Miyazaki, this transnational, pre-modern viewpoint was appealing, especially as a product of the country's postwar era and the tensions between Japanese tradition and its ties to the past, and the push to reject militarism and pursue rapid economic growth. This vision of a past more integrated with nature seemed to offer a revivifying alternative to Miyazaki's imagination.

For all of Miyazaki's love of aircraft, the era in which Miyazaki grew up bore terrible scars from technological advances, chief among them the horrors of modern war and the fiery apocalypse unleashed by the Allied forces through both atomic bombs and carpet-bombing, amply represented in the work of both Miyazaki and his Studio Ghibli co-head Isao Takahata.

↦
Three Japanese victims of
Minamata disease protest against
industrial pollution during the
United Nations Conference on
the Environment in 1972

But as the country picked up the pieces and soon rebuilt entire industries in the comparative calm of peacetime, a new disaster came to light: the ongoing dumping of methylmercury into the sea by the Chisso Corporation, leading to thousands of excruciating cases of poisoning and death. Minamata disease was recognized in 1956, but in fact the dumping had begun in the 1930s and continued into the late 1960s, as victims were deceived into thinking the dumping had stopped in 1959. The small fishing port of Minamata became a flashpoint for Japan's environmental movement and a potent signifier for the wages of modern industry, a saga that Miyazaki must have witnessed unfolding as a student growing up.

In a 1985 conversation for the *Asahi Journal* with Ernest Callenbach – author of the utopian novel *Ecotopia* and founding editor of *Film Quarterly* – Miyazaki confirmed that the Minamata poisoning inspired *Nausicaä of the Valley of the Wind*. In the future envisioned in the film, which takes place a thousand years after a devastating war, a Sea of Decay harbours a toxic forest of flora and enormous mutant bugs known as Ohmu. Initially, the humans who eke out survival on the polluted planet believe the toxicity emanates from the flora, but by the end of the film Nausicaä learns that the poison was left by the industrial effluvia of a previous civilization.

The glacial scale of time suggested by this history reflects the insidiously persistent nature of chemical pollution and perhaps also of nuclear fallout, and Miyazaki's greatest admiration in the film might be reserved for the resilient Ohmu, whom Nausicaä is able to understand beyond their perception as an inscrutable menace. The ferment of reckless industry and environmentalist movements is also a common soil from which Frank Herbert grew *Dune* (1965), to which *Nausicaä* has been compared.

⇡ Devastation in the city of Miyako, Japan, caused by the tsunamis resulting from the 2011 earthquake

⇡ Tsunami floods at the shores of Iwaki after the 2011 earthquake

⇡ Massive flooding ensues when Ponyo turns into a human, upending the natural order

Princess Mononoke is set in an entirely different era, centuries in the other direction, around the fifteenth-century Muromachi Period, which is when Miyazaki believes a Japanese national sensibility coalesced. Yet in many ways it revisits and restages the negotiation between humanity and nature seen in *Nausicaä*, whose visual style gives it more the mood of a modish dystopia redolent of the decade than the firmly Ghibli-esque realms of nature in *Princess Mononoke*.

Both films begin with a valiant young warrior consulting with elders about the course of action for dealing with a threat to the community, and indeed the focus is again on figuring out what is ailing the natural world and what sort of equilibrium can be found. It emerges that Lady Eboshi, steely leader of an ironworks town, is bent on clearing the nearby forest for mining, which leads her to hubristic attempts to subdue the forest spirits. The war with the enraged boar god and his followers shows how Miyazaki avoids treating nature as fragile or even wholly noble (while also complicating Lady Eboshi as a villain by making her a liberator of oppressed people, a group of rescued prostitutes who run the ironworks).

Again and again, Miyazaki shows nature as invaluable, irreplaceable, but also fearsome and wild. 'This world doesn't exist just for humans,'[21] he once said about Totoro's land, and this attitude persists in the sylvan battlefields of *Princess Mononoke*. There is violence, some of it quite harrowing (decapitations, grotesque curses), but also, as in *Nausicaä*, a potential for regeneration that exists independently of human aid or predation. It's possible to argue, as some critics do, that Miyazaki tends towards an apocalyptic view of the world, to be followed by renewal, and indeed that sense returned later with *Ponyo*, ostensibly an eccentric reworking of Andersen's 'The Little Mermaid'. While part of the film involves Ponyo's weird evolution from fish into girl, and her growing bond with a human boy, her magic also results in the moon and ocean falling out of joint, leading to massive flooding. The tenor of the G-rated film is much different from the wounded pathos of *Princess Mononoke* – during the flooding, people can breathe underwater thanks to magic – but there's still a distinct sense of forces beyond human control or ken.

Indeed, the visual imagination of *Ponyo* proved to be uncannily prescient. Japan's other defining modern environmental disaster occurred a few years after the film's release: the 11 March 2011 earthquake, which in turn sparked tsunamis and the Fukushima nuclear meltdowns, leading to the deaths of at least 19,000 people. Later the event would probably influence Miyazaki's rumbling depiction of the Great Kanto Earthquake in 1923 in *The Wind Rises*. But at the time Miyazaki was assisting with his son Goro's film, *From Up on Poppy Hill* (2011), and he participated in charity efforts for the earthquake as the studio paused work because of electricity outages. It was a dramatic, real-world example of the incomprehensible power and autonomy of nature that Miyazaki had depicted so often: at one moment an ecological wonder in which humans could carve out an existence, hopefully without injuring it with chemicals and the like, and at another a terrifying force more indifferent than cruel.

Leaping Panels

Miyazaki's Path
Through Manga
to Animation

If Miyazaki grew up in an era marked by a historic environmental disaster and bewildering postwar growth, his upbringing also paralleled an explosion in an art form that seemed tailor-made for a boy with a vivid imagination and keen visual sense. Manga had proliferated in newspapers in the 1920s but with the end of the Second World War came the rise of cheap *akahon* manga in the distinctive red books. Scrolled art forms such as Katsushika Hokusai's *Hokusai Manga* from the nineteenth century predated these panelled narratives, but the compact, peppy manga became a dominant form of popular entertainment in its own right, boosted early by borrowings from comics. Born in 1928 and already a rising star in his late teens, Osamu Tezuka was responsible for the legendary Astro Boy, a rocket-booted robot tyke with a greased-up cowlick befitting the mascot of American Bob's Big Boy restaurants. Other artists that Miyazaki encountered include Soji Yamakawa, Sanpei Shirato and Tetsuji Fukushima, whose science fiction manga serial *Sabaku no Maō* (*Devil of the Desert*) he came to love over and above *Astro Boy*.

As a boy in the early 1950s, Miyazaki religiously read Tezuka's mangas, including yarns such as *X-Point in the South Pacific*, about a scientist in the 'Republic of Cosmopolitan' who wants to test a new 'air bomb' on a remote island (not unlike what the United States would be attempting). The work of Tezuka and others offered solace to a self-described anxious, uncertain child: 'The few times I truly felt free were times when, for example, I read Tezuka's manga,' he said.[22] In high school, Miyazaki felt the creative tug to create mangas himself. The more serious *gekiga*-style manga fascinated him with their brooding cynicism, which he associated with the grim pasts of the manga artists who avoided happy endings that did not reflect the depredation of recent history.

Yet, as so often with Miyazaki, his resistance to a prevailing norm would clarify and define his own vision: 'Do I really want to draw gekiga,' he remembers asking himself, 'I thought it might be better to express in an honest way that what is good is good, what is pretty is pretty, and what is beautiful is beautiful.'[23] The catalyst for this realization was nothing other than the 1958 animated film, *Hakujaden* (aka *Panda and the Magic Serpent*), Japan's first such feature, suggesting that even early on, the moving-image appeal to Miyazaki and awakened a dynamic sensibility within him.

At university – where Miyazaki joined a children's literature study club for lack of a manga study club – he drew manga in the thousands of pages and submitted some to publishers in the rental-library market. But upon graduation in 1963, perhaps sensing the potential for the newer field of animation in Japan, he joined Toei Animation and committed to his work as an animator. No doubt the space-age dynamism of *Astro Boy* percolated in Miyazaki's mind as he animated the likes of *Gulliver's Travels Beyond the Moon* (1965), though at this point he was still working for the cut-out-like vision of another director. In later years, however, he would remain devoted to this godfather of the manga, calling himself still 'in the spell of Tezuka-san for drawing,'[24] even as he lambasted the chintzy *Astro Boy* animations that were rushed to television.

↑ Tradesmen and entertainers, from the
first volume of the *Hokusai Manga* (1814)
by Katsushika Hokusai

↑ A re-creation of a desk in the Tokiwaso
apartment building that was home to
prominent manga artists such as
Osamu Tezuka in the 1950s and 60s

↑ Assorted covers of *Astro Boy*, the pioneering
manga illustrated by Osamu Tezuka

As a young key animator, Miyazaki was soon assigned to create promotional manga adaptations of the films he worked on, such as serializations of *Puss 'n Boots* and *Animal Treasure Island*. At one point he even published a weekly manga called *People of the Desert* under a pseudonym. But the fullest flowering of his manga exploits wouldn't come until he had already directed his debut feature, *Lupin III: The Castle of Cagliostro*, and would also connect him with his future collaborator, Toshio Suzuki, a co-editor of *Animage* magazine. After *Animage* devoted an issue to Miyazaki in August 1981, he began serializing his *Nausicaä of the Valley of the Wind* manga in its February 1982 issue (while also, typically enough for the draw-till-you-drop industry, directing a few episodes of the TV series *Sherlock Hound*).

The following year, production began on *Nausicaä* the film, but Miyazaki would not finish the serialized manga, incredibly, until March 1994, returning to it even after the all-consuming work of his features and the founding of Studio Ghibli. The depth and detail are astonishing, with the black-and-white panels seething with the density of a Dürer wood engraving, and the deprivation and severity of Nausicaä's world can make the film's colourful dystopia look downright pop by comparison.

If *Nausicaä* the manga feels like an obsessive masterpiece in the shadows of his increasing renown as an animator, Miyazaki's opinion of the manga landscape at large was increasingly sceptical. What had been a subculture – he remembers being the only kid in his high school reading mangas – now seemed pervasive, and to him the starting point for too much popular culture in Japan generally.

His diagnosis was withering and, once again, it caused him to redouble his commitment to the moving image and its alchemy of time and space: 'Films must hold on to their space, to their tenacious expression as films. In current Japanese culture, everything has become insubstantial and mangalike, with all the cuts angles and actors as shallow as graphic novels.'[25] While he retained a kind of grudging admiration for the purity of some *shōjo* (young girl) manga, his features grew only more ambitious and powerful in their provocative ambivalence, as with *Princess Mononoke*. Yet he clearly still drew on manga when it suited his purposes: a fan of Daijiro Morohoshi's *Mud Men*, serialized from 1975 to 1982, he drew on its renderings of the Asaro tribe in Papua New Guinea, whose face paint and masks are strongly echoed in *Princess Mononoke*.

Yet manga remained a fertile sketchbook art form for Miyazaki, even in the thick of his career. Consider his *Daydream* series of notes and sketches, or *The Age of the Flying Boat* series that essentially became *Porco Rosso*, or *The Wind Rises* manga that fed into that film. Manga seems to be a playground for Miyazaki to indulge his obsessions in the manner of someone tinkering in his study. That includes the wonky military history of his two little-remarked mangas about German tanks in the Second World War: one about a fictional mechanic seeking to defect; another about the real-life commander Otto Carius.

For all Miyazaki's dedication to the art of motion, one can also sense in his heart the up-all-night illustrator at a desk, who playfully draws himself, in manga comics, as a blustering pig.

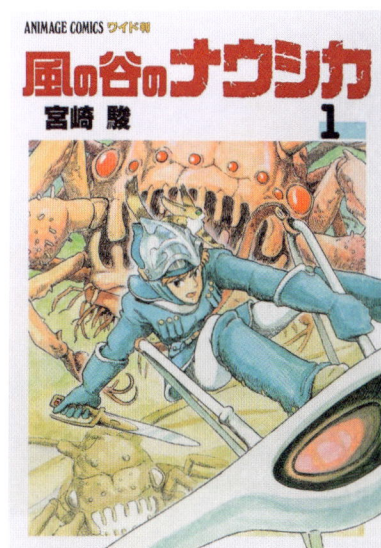

↥ *Nausicaä of the Valley of the Wind* manga, in the first volume collecting the chapters originally published serially

Moveable Feasts

The Foods that Infuse Scenes with Feeling

Like many filmmakers, Miyazaki is occasionally asked which movies he likes, and on at least two occasions the answer has been somewhat unexpected: *Babette's Feast*. The 1987 Danish movie won an Oscar for its story of a Parisian refugee in Denmark who assembles the titular banquet of French cuisine – and if any clue existed to why the film leapt to Miyazaki's mind, it might be the lavish, multicourse spread that's its delectable centrepiece. Some of Miyazaki's most memorable, and even emotional, moments are food scenes, which tend to be fashioned with loving detail and a knack for triggering a Pavlovian response in viewers. Where other animated movies gloss over the details of food, or forget to include them as central to human connection, Miyazaki brings warmth and an ethos of care to even the simplest of meals. One can imagine him recalling his father's comfort-food specialties, when his mother was sick, which included dried mackerel, *kusaya* (fermented fish) and sardines in the processed form of *tatami iwashi*.

Despite the outlandish stories in his films, Miyazaki derives many of his food choices from the fondly familiar rituals of Japanese family life. One of the most beloved such meals occurs in *My Neighbor Totoro*: lunch prepared by the older sister, Satsuki, who regularly takes care of her younger sister, Mei, especially as their father is preoccupied with their mother's illness and his work. Satsuki assembles a red bento box for her father and sister, placing delectable homey ingredients: *sakura denbu*, a pink condiment made from cod, a pile of green soybeans and a pickled plum (*umeboshi*) atop a fluffy bed of rice. It's a standard meal that can't help but also resemble a gift, neatly put together, and in that sense Satsuki's bento box has its echo later on when Mei becomes fixated on presenting an ear of corn to her mother. The corn is not a meal – it's green, not even shucked – but you can feel the love that Mei has invested into this food item, which she probably doesn't know how to prepare yet. Scratched into the wrapping: 'To Mom'.

A similar, differently poignant exchange takes place in *Kiki's Delivery Service*, when the intrepid young witch befriends an elderly woman on one of her deliveries. Kiki helps the woman bake a herring and pumpkin potpie in a wood-fire oven for her granddaughter's birthday party, with an actual fish shape embossed on the crust and olives at the edges. It's evidently a comfort food that also feels redolent of a grandmother's slightly old-fashioned creation (which, by available evidence, Miyazaki seems to have concocted for the film). But Miyazaki puts a twist on the expected chain of kindnesses when Kiki travels to the house of the granddaughter and finds only peevish ingratitude: 'I hate grandma's stupid pies!' the young woman says, taking the pie and slamming the door. Let it never be said that Miyazaki gilds his films with treacle; the scene is consistent, though, with his tolerance of a range of wilfulness in his young characters. Later, Kiki's shock is smoothed over by a lovely gift from the grandmother: a chocolate cake decorated with her name, Kiki, and a witch on a broom. A far more grateful and indeed joyous food recipient is Ponyo, who adores the ham served in her ramen by Sosuke's mother; likewise excited are the old women at Mahito's new home, who coo over canned goods such as sardines, salmon and 'corned beef'.

↥ *Babette's Feast* (1987), a film that Miyazaki liked (and probably not coincidentally is full of food)

↥ Satsuki lovingly prepares bento boxes for her family in *My Neighbor Totoro*

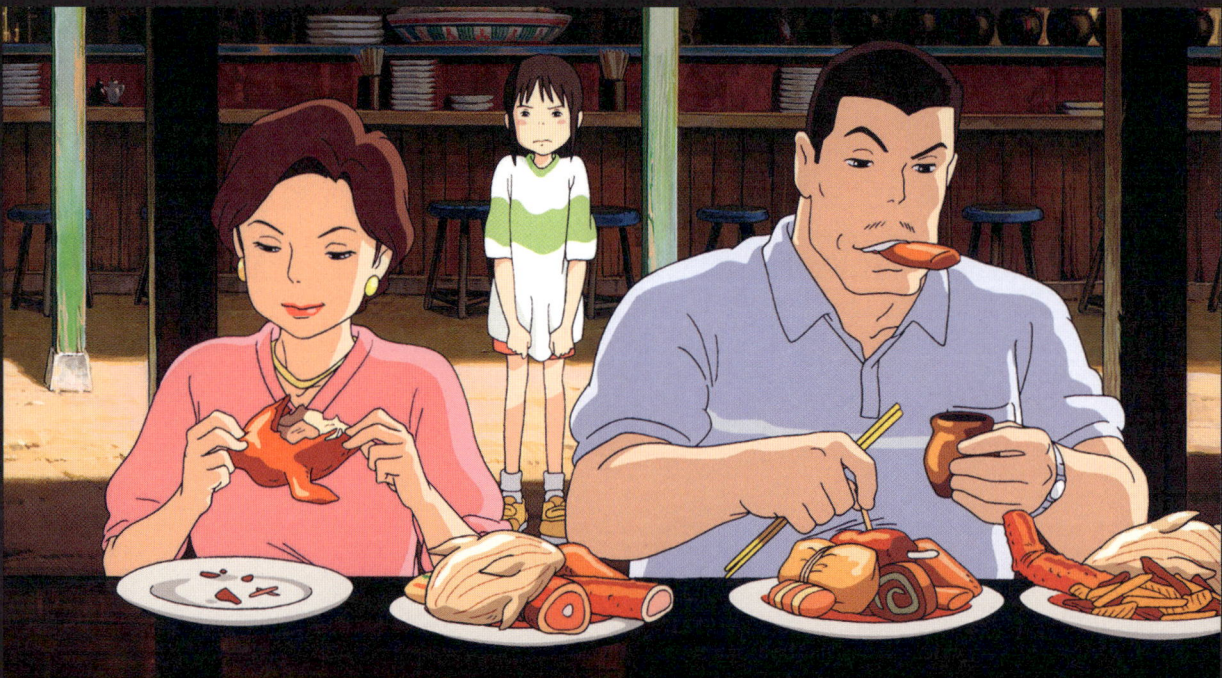

↥ Chihiro's parents pig out at a mysteriously
   unattended restaurant – a meal with
   transformative consequences – in *Spirited Away*

↥ Haku gives rice balls to Chihiro in
   a comforting gesture amid strife
   at the bathhouse in *Spirited Away*

But the Miyazaki feature most given over to food in all its uses is *Spirited Away*, where it serves every purpose from luxury service to comfort food to worker fuel. The culinary adventure begins with a nightmare: Chihiro's parents gobbling unattended fried food at a restaurant and turning into pigs. This is food as enchantment, a temptation that even a child with a passing acquaintance of fairy tales in any culture might know better than to tuck into. But with the assurance of urban foodies collecting a new restaurant, the parents start gobbling it all down, without even a server in sight to order from or pay. Sample fare: dumplings, a quail-like bird and a mass resembling balled-up noodles that one Ghibli employee later identified as 'stomach of coelacanth' – an ancient fish and, hence, probably a delicacy reserved for spirits, rather than humans, to consume.

Later on, as Chihiro gets mired in the labyrinthine protocols of the bathhouse and missing her family, she shares bean buns with a mentoring co-worker, and has a meaningful meal of her own outside: an *onigiri* (rice ball) offered by her mysterious guide, Haku. With a bite of this humble morsel, the distressed young girl bursts into tears, as Miyazaki taps a sense memory as common as comfort food and here as potent as any magic in the movie.

The boiler room in *Spirited Away*, with its spider-like Kamaji for a stoker and custodian, is an example of Miyazaki's depictions of food and drink. Kamaji slurps his tea from a rounded teapot that resembles those of the Edo Period, as if suggesting that he's been at this job for a considerable length of time. The soot sprites who ferry coal into the stove receive a distinctive treat as a reward for their work (or perhaps as a kind of feed or fuel to keep them going): *konpeito*, colourful star-bursts of candy. This sugary sweet dates back to the arrival of Portuguese traders in the sixteenth century but became an ingrained part of the Japanese repertoire of candies. Western food staples crop up in *Laputa: Castle in the Sky* – an egg sandwich – and in *Howl's Moving Castle*, too: the fried egg from the impromptu castle breakfast, based on Miyazaki's memory of cooking cheap as a student. (Touchingly, the animator bought a chunk of bacon to practise drawing it.)

When including specifically Japanese foods, Miyazaki is often helping to shade in a bit of period detail. In *The Wind Rises*, for example, the aeroplane designer Jiro buys two Siberia sponge cakes at a bakery. Identifiable by its dark stripe, this confection sandwiches bean paste jelly between two pieces of *castella* (sponge cake). The cake seems to have appeared in Japanese bakeries during the late Meiji Period to the Taishō Period, fading away by the end of the Second World War – effectively stamping the scene as a memory in the making.

It is food, in fact, that is a catalyst for Jiro's aircraft design. Picking his way through a meal of *saba misoni* – mackerel in miso and ginger – in a cafeteria, he plucks and holds up a bone. The curve presents a naturally elegant, aerodynamic solution for the wing strut of a fighter plane – out of nourishment, a clue for a beautiful flying machine of death.

↑ A glazed, rounded teapot from the Edo Period, similar to what you might see in Kamaji's boiler room in *Spirited Away*

CHAPTER FIVE

SONGS
OF
INNOCENCE
AND
EXPERIENCE

The Personal Memories That Haunt
(and Cheer Up) Miyazaki's Movies

PART ONE

Mamma Miyazaki

His First and Fiercest Muse

'The Miyazaki bloodline seems to lack a certain quality of submission to others,' Shirou Miyazaki wrote in a 1990 family reminiscence about his brother, published in Studio Ghibli's book about *Laputa: Castle in the Sky*. Hayao was the second-eldest of four brothers, and Shirou was the youngest, born to Yoshiko and Katsuji Miyazaki. Katsuji and especially his father before him, who founded the family business in manufacturing, were formidable presences. Yet Shirou's deadpan comment perhaps most aptly describes Miyazaki's mother, Yoshiko, the woman at the heart of his indomitable drive and curiosity, and perhaps the guiding spirit behind his energetic young female protagonists and the shrewd, independent older women who are just as striking in his films.

Yoshiko had to be indomitable herself, raising four sons during wartime and beyond under debilitating circumstances. 'My three brothers and I were no match for her,' Hayao remembers.[26] She suffered from spinal tuberculosis, or Pott disease, which causes severe back pain and neurological dysfunction, a condition that left her bedridden for a nine-year period from 1947. Hayao was at that point around six years of age, and he would have seen his mother nearly unable to move except for her hands and head, at first in hospital for several years of treatment and then at home, recovering while wrapped in plaster. The young Miyazaki, who was introverted and interested in books and drawing, enjoyed having complex conversations with his cosmopolitan mother, who was well-versed in culture, politics, economics and so on. She gave her son, among other books, a copy of Genzaburo Yoshino's *How Do You Live?* – the book Mahito finds in his room, left by his mother, in *The Boy and the Heron*, illustrated with an engraving of Jean-François Millet's *The Sower* (1851).

However, one does not need to wait until the 2023 release of *The Boy and the Heron* to find a Rosebud for Miyazaki's loving reverence for his mother. An acknowledged tribute to Yoshiko appears in *Laputa: Castle in the Sky*, Miyazaki's very first feature released under the Studio Ghibli banner. It was also the first feature he directed since Yoshiko Miyazaki died three years earlier at the age of 71. One of the two formidable foes pursuing Pazu and Sheeta, the two young protagonists, is a character who instantly feels as if she could headline her own film or series: Dola, captain of the air pirate gang trying to swipe Sheeta's treasure. Flamboyant, rascally, funny, brave and shrewd, she is the pigtailed mother-boss to three sons and numerous cronies, barking orders and whipping the bumbling crew into shape for air battles and other missions. Despite the men's testosterone-fuelled swagger and flourishes – bushy moustaches, or a dainty Clark Gable pencil-style for one – they keep their eyes peeled for Dola and snap into action when caught dithering. Sometimes she is 'Captain'; other times they just call her 'Mom'.

↑ *The Sower* (1851) by Jean-François Millet, which features
in the copy of *How Do You Live?* that Mahito's mother
leaves behind for him in *The Boy and the Heron*

Mei and Satsuki's
visit to their mother
in hospital in *My
Neighbor Totoro*
evokes Miyazaki's
love for his own
ailing mother

Young Sophie is
transformed into
a granny in *Howl's
Moving Castle*

It's easy to picture Miyazaki's mother wrangling five men – four sons and her husband – with their own headstrong attitudes, and imagine her action-adventure avatar as Dola. Shirou Miyazaki certainly did: 'I hope you associate [our mother] with Dola, the female pirate in *Laputa*,' he wrote in his 1990 text. Dola and other such depictions have led some critics to describe Miyazaki's movies as feminist in featuring strong female characters in powerful roles, throughout different historical backdrops and fantastical settings, from Nausicaä to Yubaba in *Spirited Away* to Lady Eboshi in *Princess Mononoke*.

But in his work Miyazaki also commemorates, and works though, the pain and poignancy of his mother's illness and how it affected her relationships with her children. In the next feature Miyazaki directed, *My Neighbor Totoro*, the mother of Satsuki and Mei is convalescing in a hospital, just as Yoshiko Miyazaki did in Shichikokuyama. The absence of the sisters' mother is keenly felt but also sets the stage for their wanderings and encounters with spirits in nature, while their father works or tends to errands or visits his wife. (The dusty house also evokes the home where the Miyazaki family moved after the war.) The echo recurs in *The Wind Rises*, in which Jiro's wife suffers from tuberculosis, an element that Miyazaki blends into the story of this aircraft engineer, from the novel *The Wind Rises* (1937) by Tatsuo Hori.

Miyazaki's cinematic tribute to his mother is therefore two-sided: not just the whirlwind energy of a canny Dola or Yubaba (who's also explicitly a mum in *Spirited Away*), but also a love irrevocably marked by illness and absence. This duality is one of many signs of Miyazaki's resistance to pure escapism in his work; he holds on to the ache as well as the pleasure, fundamentally staying true to what must have been very distinct eras in his mother's life. In that sense Sophie, the young haberdasher in *Howl's Moving Castle*, becomes an intriguing amalgam of two of Miyazaki's archetypes: aspirational young women and their canny elders. She is transformed by a curse into a much older woman, but she also comes to appreciate the advantages in perspective age can bring. Is the leap in years perhaps Miyazaki's intuitive understanding of how his mother may have felt post-illness, finding herself looking at a changed world nearly a decade older? Some have also speculated it's a tribute to Miyazaki's wife, Akemi Ota, a fellow animator at Toei who married him in 1965, but left her career and gave up years to raise their children while her husband worked.

In the documentary *10 Years with Hayao Miyazaki*, the animator speaks about his mother with a touching candour that perhaps sheds more light on how his feelings about her enter his work. Working on *Ponyo* in his late sixties, he is already musing on how many years he has left. In one scene, he listens to a tape of longtime collaborator Joe Hisaishi's score, visibly tearing up and wiping his eyes. One line seems to access a memory from deep within: 'I want to dance once more'. 'I can't help recalling my mother,' Miyazaki says, wondering aloud how she could have lived her life more fully. It's easy to think of his animations as a kind of realization of unfulfilled dreams, but his complicated films also bear out the fullness of life, the sadness and the joy both creating who you are.

Appetite for Destruction

How the Second World
War Shapes and Breaks
Miyazaki's Universe

For a director whose most famous character is a big furry spirit whose favourite occupations are napping and dancing around plants, visions of war and destruction crop up quite a bit in the films of Miyazaki. It's practically inescapable: *Nausicaä* opens in a desolate post-nuclear landscape where fresh conflict is always on the march. *Princess Mononoke* stages a terrifying battle royale between animal spirits and human beings, with thundering mobilizations and grisly killings and injuries along the way. In *Howl's Moving Castle* the titular warlock sails over firestorms, and even the roguish *Porco Rosso* has a haunting flashback to a vast procession of ghostly aircraft ascending to plane heaven, the myriad casualties of untold air battles. Not just death, but war, is a part of life in Miyazaki's worlds.

War, in fact, was part of Miyazaki's life, too, as seems inevitable for anyone who was born in Japan during the Second World War. But supplying the Japanese war effort was the family business: the company Miyazaki Airplane – where Hayao's father Katsuji worked for his uncle – built rudders, fan belts and other parts for Nakajima Aircraft, manufacturers of the Mitsubishi A6M Zero fighter plane. The Zero (famously used in the Pearl Harbor attack) is the very same plane on which Jiro Horikoshi, the protagonist of *The Wind Rises*, was the chief engineer. When Miyazaki's immediate family relocated during 1944–46 to Utsunomiya (where his grandfather had an estate), it was not only to escape the firebombing of Tokyo 100 kilometres (60 miles) south; Utsunomiya was also where many industries, including Nakajima Aircraft, had relocated. This concentration of industries and an army presence eventually made Utsunomiya a target of Allied bombing as well in 1945, and almost half of the city was destroyed.

Born on 4 January 1941, Miyazaki was four years old and remembers the barrage and the fires. They still burn in his films. *The Boy and the Heron* opens with what could be a personal flashback: air raid sirens going off and waking a boy up in the middle of the night, glowing cinders floating eerily, fires in the distance. In the film, Mahito runs at full tilt through the street, weaving among passers-by, in search of his mother's hospital which is on fire; after a cut, it's suddenly day and Imperial tanks roll through the streets. Later, a small procession holds banners: 'May your luck last long in battle' and 'Congratulations on your call-up'. War is in the air, and, like Miyazaki's family, Mahito's father brings him from Tokyo to the countryside where he has a 'new factory'. As the voiceover explains: 'Three years into the war, mother died. A year later, my father and I left Tokyo.' When Mahito falls asleep for the first time in his new home (whose sprawl perhaps echoes his grandfather's estate), he dreams of the fires again, and his mother rising and fading away like a phantom.

Like *The Boy and the Heron*, *The Wind Rises* plunges the viewer into the dream life of its protagonist to such an extent that feelings and memories and visions become inextricably bound. It seems another instance of Miyazaki working through the recurring themes of trauma, both wartime Japan generally and the disease that held back his mother. The link to wartime Japan is clear in choosing actual Zero engineer Jiro Horikoshi as a subject, but Miyazaki melds details of Horikoshi's biography with elements from *The Wind Rises* by Tatsuo Hori, whom Miyazaki also imitates in mining Hori's citation from Paul Valéry's poem 'Le cimetière marin' ('The Graveyard by the Sea'):

The wind rises
We must try to live.

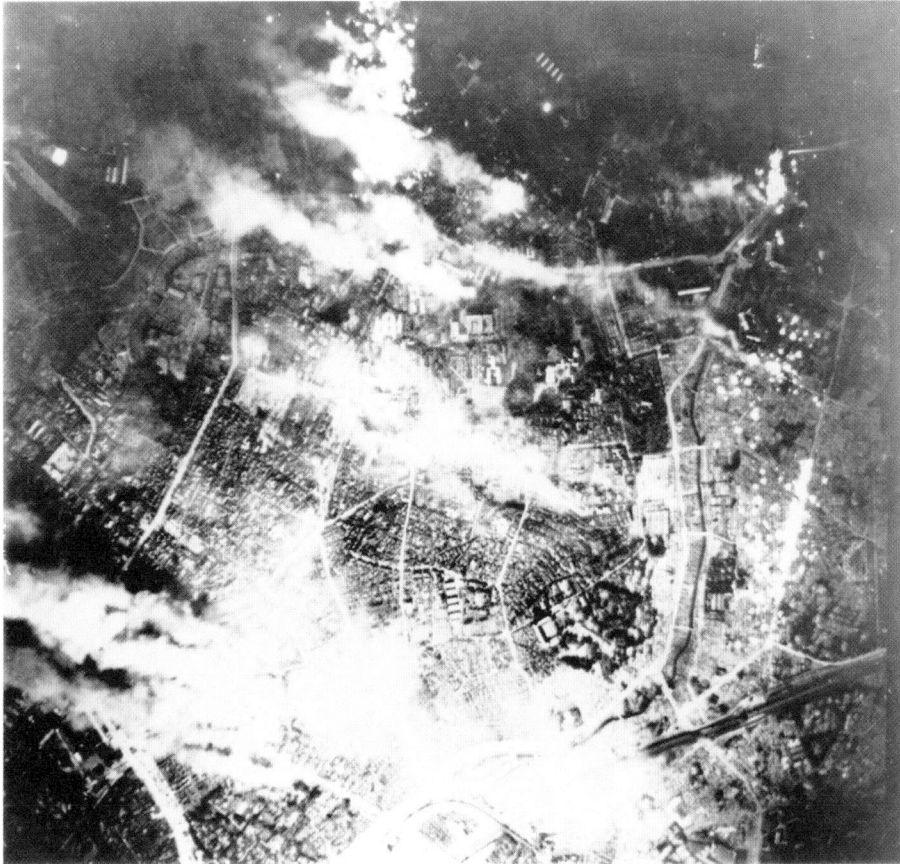

⬆ Aerial view of Tokyo burning under assault
   by American B-29 bombers on 26 May 1945

⬆ The aftermath of the deadly Operation
   Meetinghouse bombing raid of Tokyo in
   March 1945 undertaken by the United States

⇧ Jiro inspects planes in *The Wind Rises*, which incorporates details from the life of the engineer who developed Japan's Zero fighter in the Second World War

⇧ Sophie looks at a street in flames after bombing during the war in *Howl's Moving Castle*

↑   Naoko, Jiro's future wife,
    painting in *The Wind Rises*

In Hori's story, a writer at a hotel meets a woman who is working on a painting and who is later joined by her father; similarly, Miyazaki's Jiro meets his future wife, Naoko, at a summer resort where his superiors have sent him to recharge, and she too paints and has a watchful father. Miyazaki continues the borrowing when Naoko must go to a sanatorium, as indeed happens for Hori's couple. (He's aided at the resort by a German exile, Castorp, named after the protagonist of Thomas Mann's sanatorium novel *The Magic Mountain*.) Hori in turn drew upon his own life: his spouse died of tuberculosis, as indeed he would at 48.

In a sense the narrative amalgam of *The Wind Rises* suggests that Miyazaki is making a dual portrait drawn from the lives of his parents: both mother and father, making the most of the time together when they had it, amid the pressures and separations of war and disease.

If *The Wind Rises* feels like a film more directed at adults than the mingled audiences of Miyazaki's other films, perhaps that's because this dual portrait reflects the perspective of an older artist looking back and identifying more with his parents than with himself as a child. That perspective might matter little to critics who object that Jiro, and by extension Miyazaki, seem insufficiently concerned with the use of his plane designs for warfare by Imperial Japan. But Miyazaki clearly draws on his own parents' compartmentalized experience, and depicts not the greater glory of the fascist state but an engineer's idealized dream of flight detached from reality and ultimately doomed. Miyazaki seems to have little patience for people's inquisitiveness about his interest in the Second World War: 'I'm fascinated by wars, and I read a lot about them,' he said in a 1994 interview published in *YOMU*.

'People therefore often ask me, "Miyazaki-san, do you like war?" and I respond by asking if they think AIDS researchers like AIDS.'[27]

Remarkably, a few months after *The Wind Rises* was released, a film titled *The Eternal Zero* set box office records in Japan with the story of a kamikaze fighter and the grandson who learns about his life. Miyazaki promptly criticized the film as rife with fabrication and perpetrating an established 'phony myth' about the nobility of such pilots. His very next film, *The Boy and the Heron*, returns to the 1940s – possibly even interlocking with the time frame of *The Wind Rises* – and shows Mahito's father managing groups working on giant aeroplane parts, much as Miyazaki's father did. But the animator has gone back to the drawing board, as it were, and returned the point of view to that of a wartime child, who is stunned by the death of his mother and working it all out in a world of fantasy and dreams.

P
A
R
T
  T
  H
  R
  E
  E

Young and Restless

The Children at the Heart of Miyazaki's Art

Some of the most touching moments in Miyazaki's work are those that feel recognizable from daily life, in more peaceful times. One such moment takes place near the end of *My Neighbor Totoro*, when the children are finally able to visit their mother in the hospital (with assistance from the Catbus). Sitting with her two daughters, she begins to brush Satsuki's hair, saying how much she reminds her of herself at her age, which brings a smile to the girl's face. The tender exchange is the kind of bonding moment many women and girls might relate to – routine and yet special too. Miyazaki has two sons and came from a family of all men except for his mother, but he recognized the importance of such a moment. And, remarkably, he has connected it to a story told in passing by a co-worker, about a sick friend who had brushed her child's hair while talking to her, much as happens for Satsuki.

One has the sense of Miyazaki as a sensitive watcher and listener of the world around him, with his antennae up for the precise details that make a moment feel real and singularly human, even in the context of fantasy. In the case of the children in his films, that sometimes means drawing upon his own sense memories, many of which course through *My Neighbor Totoro*. The absence of the sisters' mother leads to all sorts of habits that come straight out of Miyazaki's recollections of coming home from school to an empty house and feeling a loneliness he couldn't yet express. When his mother was in hospital, he recalls having to make meals and clean up, while another brother would do the shopping and heat the bath; indeed, Satsuki puts together bento boxes for her temporarily single-parent family.

The echoes extend even to major plot points. The final third of the film hinges on Mei going missing when she and Satsuki have a spat over not being able to visit their mother. In a fit of pique and perhaps a desire to will a visit into being, Mei insists on journeying solo to deliver a corn cob to their mother. Two memories are at work here in Miyazaki's imagination. One is when a little brother went astray after a family trip to a festival, leading to a collective panic that they would not be able to locate him. (They did, in a resolution that nearly conjures up a Miyazakian image: the boy was found clinging to a somewhat bewildered senior citizen, who simply towed him along on her walk.) The corn cob mission also has a clear precursor in Miyazaki's own childhood, when he went to summer school at the seaside and, upon seeing a sea urchin, was consumed with the joyful urge to show it to his mother. He held on to it, and of course it spoilt; no doubt his mother already knew what a sea urchin looked like. But Miyazaki channels this zeal and sense of mission from decades earlier to create a winning and poignant picture of his character's emotional state.

↑ In *My Neighbor Totoro*, Satsuki hugs her younger sister, Mei, who went missing, as the Catbus grins in the background

↑ Chihiro mopes in her parents' car on the way to their new home at the start of *Spirited Away*

←
Kiki's boredom at the bakery where she works leads to her starting her own business in *Kiki's Delivery Service*

←
Miyazaki chose to portray two sisters in *My Neighbor Totoro* as a deliberate contrast to his own two sons

Miyazaki has two sons, born in 1967 and 1969, and has said he chose to portray two sisters in *My Neighbor Totoro* partly to avoid connecting the film too much with his own children. But when it comes to the sprightly protagonists in other films, he has been freely inspired by the children of friends and colleagues. The teenage heroine of *Kiki's Delivery Service* was partly inspired by the daughter of Toshio Suzuki, his producer and collaborator, though Miyazaki has said he also drew on the habits of the young female animators who he trained at Studio Ghibli as new hires. For Chihiro in *Spirited Away*, Miyazaki thought of the 10-year-old daughter of a colleague, whose family had visited the director at a country house every summer. In this case, Miyazaki has spoken of particular details – how the girl could run a certain way, like Chihiro does, or how she interacted with adults. He has a sense of humour and ownership about the headstrong character he created – 'The girl's a brat, frankly,' he joked at a press conference for the film[28] – but his dedication to his child characters runs deep: jibe aside, Chihiro is depicted as having deep wells of compassion that regularly teach spirits and humans alike a lesson by example.

Part of what makes Miyazaki's cinematic children so vivid is how they feel tailored to particular phases in a child's life. Chihiro may be dealing with river spirits and witches and a baffling system of bathhouse tokens, but she's also generally coming into her own as a budding, independent child. As Miyazaki put it so memorably years before making *Spirited Away*, speaking of being 10 years of age: 'It's the time of life when you become the main character in your own story.'[29] (Later on, she'll even have to save her own parents after they've turned into pigs, in a sequence influenced by Otfried Preussler's novel *Krabat*.) Likewise, the titular fish-girl of *Ponyo* has many hallmarks of a strong-willed toddler, and indeed Miyazaki modelled this pint-sized force of nature on Fuki, the small daughter of Katsuya Kondō, a character designer Miyazaki works with. In the documentary *10 Years with Hayao Miyazaki*, the director is shown enjoying photos of little Fuki, whose energy and force of personality indeed leap off the page. It's easy to find echoes in one photograph of Fuki, arms outstretched and mouth open wide in a laugh, to Ponyo impulsively running and hugging her human friend Sosuke.

Like many artists who have children, Miyazaki feels that his sons have indelibly influenced his choice of subject. He's said that he doubted he would have wanted to make films for children if he hadn't become a parent himself. And, indeed, each of these characters also reflect a parent's attention to a child's point of view, whether it's Ponyo encountering the human world (how will my son respond to new people and things?) or Kiki striking out on her own in a new town (how will my son fare with building his own career?). As inventive as the settings and scenarios may be, Miyazaki gives them resonance by looking to the universal experiences of family.

Workplace World

How the Studio Ghibli Office Informs *Spirited Away*

For an admitted workaholic like Hayao Miyazaki, the office can become like a second family, and perhaps the animation industry is an especially strong example of that. Unlike the production of live-action films, which are typically filmed in different locations, the creation of an animated feature centres upon the studio, and when the company is Studio Ghibli, a core team of animators and designers can be assembled under a single roof. A number of documentaries have been made about Studio Ghibli and Miyazaki (e.g. *10 Years with Hayao Miyazaki*, *The Kingdom of Dreams and Madness*, 2013, *How Princess Mononoke Was Born*, 1998), and a reliable pleasure of their chronicles is getting to watch Miyazaki in his element at the office.

The man has his routines: he sweats at his desk over finding inspiration or getting a gesture just right, he stalks the halls to find someone (or, in one case, to avoid his son, Goro, during the making of *From Up on Poppy Hill*), he blows off steam by joking around with employees. Other workers we see are mostly quietly busy in their cubicles, though producer Toshio Suzuki is a recurring 'character' of sorts, managing timelines and gently nudging Miyazaki on one or another outstanding issue.

This overview of the Studio Ghibli workplace is worth sketching because Miyazaki naturally dramatizes or expresses aspects in his movies. It's another way in which *The Wind Rises*, for example, is a deeply personal film, though it's not often acknowledged as it frequently overlaps with family history. On one level, the film is a tribute to the process of creation at Studio Ghibli. When Jiro Horikoshi goes to work for the Mitsubishi Corporation as a young engineer, he must find solutions to aeronautic challenges, design blueprints, take into account criticism and witness test flights. The collaborative nature of the endeavour and of course the drawing up of plans at his easel evoke the teamwork and illustration that go into animation. It's also likely that Miyazaki, as the son of an aeroplane engineer, finds a natural parallel between aircraft design and animation: both involve detailed planning on the page that is then set into motion. Whether a particular animated sequence is successful artistically must feel as urgent and delicate a process to Miyazaki as whether a plane takes flight and stays aloft. That's in addition to Miyazaki's evident pleasure in, and even obsession with, aircraft of all sorts, both on screen and in comics.

But beyond the analogies to animation and engineering, one can detect a kind of workplace portraiture in *The Wind Rises*. Jiro's boss at Mitsubishi is Kurokawa, a diminutive man with a brusque manner who at first seems to have an axe to grind with his new, naive charge. He impatiently rushes around the office and certainly looks angry most of the time, mouth and eyebrows permanently downturned in a sour expression. But his eyes and his actions speak otherwise: he has a piercing focus on the project at hand, and despite seeming outwardly frustrated with Jiro's going off-assignment to pursue his own ideas, he protects him and looks out for his opportunities. He's a mentor figure, but also simply a no-nonsense guide who keeps things on track, qualities that Miyazaki clearly appreciates in the workplace, though his remorseless rigour could also evoke Miyazaki himself (at least, to judge from the tough love he displays towards his son Goro in *10 Years with Hayao Miyazaki*).

砂田麻美 監督作品

夢と狂気の王国

プロデューサー 川上量生

製作・ドワンゴ 脚本・監督・砂田麻美 音楽・高木正勝 協力・スタジオジブリ 制作・エネット 配給・東宝 2013年/日本/カラー/デジタル

yumetokyoki.com

原発の電気は
いりません

ジブリにしのび込んだ
マミちゃんの冒険。

11月16日（土）全国ロードショー

↑ Poster for *The Kingdom of Dreams and Madness*, a 2013 documentary about Studio Ghibli during the production of *The Wind Rises* and *The Tale of the Princess Kaguya*

↑ The Studio Ghibli office headquarters,
from *Never-Ending Man: Hayao Miyazaki*,
a 2016 behind-the-scenes documentary

↑ Miyazaki sketching a panel, from
Never-Ending Man: Hayao Miyazaki

↥ Miyazaki supervising (or maybe just joking with)
an employee at Studio Ghibli, from *Never-Ending
Man: Hayao Miyazaki*

↥ The Studio Ghibli team busily at work,
from *Never-Ending Man: Hayao Miyazaki*

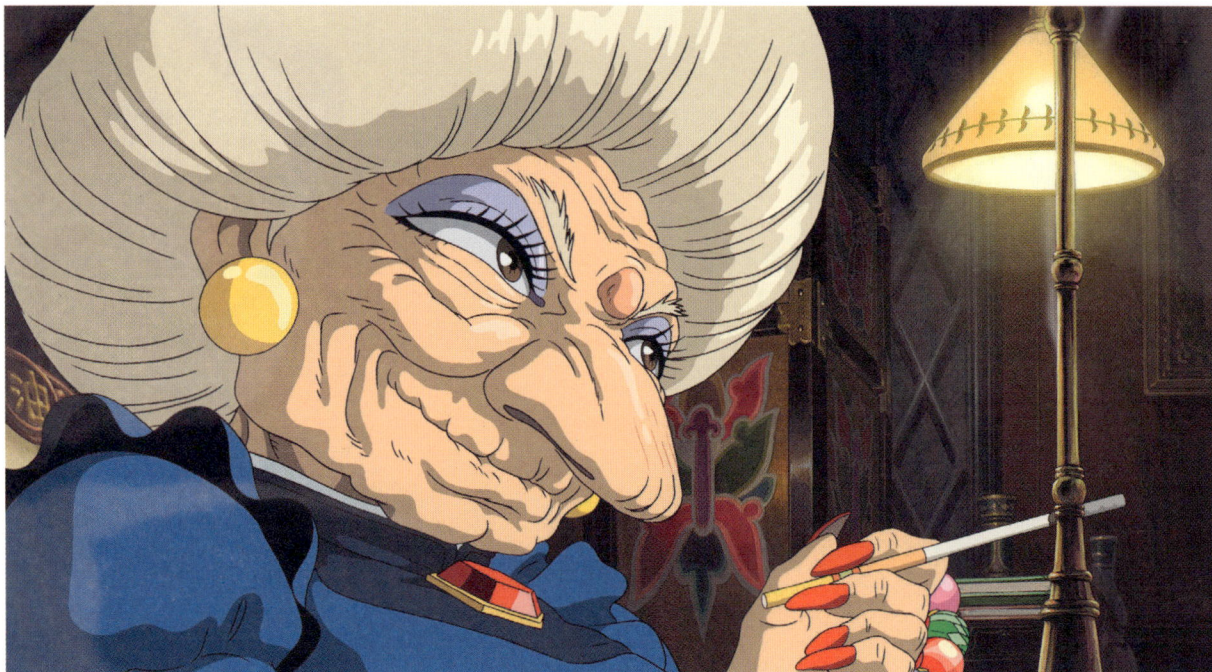

⇑ Yubaba, who runs the bathhouse in
Spirited Away, is supposedly inspired
by Studio Ghibli producer Toshio Suzuki

112

⇑ Jiro at the drafting table, overseen by his
bosses at the aircraft firm, in *The Wind Rises*

The Boy and the Heron offers another, unexpected twist on how Miyazaki's workplace finds its way into his films. In press interviews, Toshio Suzuki has maintained that a direct symbolism exists in the film's main characters: namely, that the boy, Mahito, is Miyazaki, and that the heron is none other than Suzuki. In the film, the heron is a trickster figure who leads Mahito into other realms and apparent danger, but who also ends up joining forces with the boy. In Suzuki's perhaps idealized view, this relationship tracks with the close friendship between himself and Miyazaki, to the extent that something about the boy and the heron's interactions reminded him of daily conversations at the office. Adding a further twist, Suzuki has also said that the wizard Machito encounters in *The Boy and the Heron* is an homage to another titan of Studio Ghibli, Isao Takahata, whose partnership with Miyazaki started early on *Hols: Prince of the Sun* (1968).[30] Whatever the case, there's a clear power to the workplace bonds that sustain Miyazaki and indeed make possible the large-scale projects that hinge on his imagination day to day.

As much as Miyazaki is the pivotal figure as the director, his films repeatedly reflect a belief in the collective action of the workplace, and not just its efficacy, but also the joy of it. We get a peek at this mentality early on, in *Porco Rosso*, at Piccolo's workshop which revamps Porco's beloved plane. There's a spirit of camaraderie and bustling efficiency, and also notable is that it's an all-female staff, because the men have left to find jobs elsewhere due to the Depression. The appreciation for their labour tracks with Miyazaki's mentorship of women at Studio Ghibli, and the crucial roles of women like Michiyo Yasuda, his longtime colour designer. (It's also worth noting that Miyazaki's career was made possible by his wife: Akemi was also an animator but took the lead in staying home to raise their children while Miyazaki worked.)

Perhaps the most lavish metaphor for the workplace in Miyazaki's films is *Spirited Away*, a kind of omnibus work. Legions of workers, hustling from room to room, endlessly prepare for the next outlandish spirit-guest, who will send everyone into a frenzy to get everything ready till the last minute – the bathhouse is a metaphor for an animation studio working under deadline. Twin witches Yubaba and Zeniba also represent the dual nature of the harried worker – perhaps tense and rambunctious at the office, Miyazaki believed, but relaxed at home. 'That's Japan itself', Miyazaki once said of the 'strange world' Chihiro has entered. He was referring to the dormitories of Japanese firms in decades past,[31] but he might also have been thinking of the sovereign nation of Studio Ghibli, wrangling an animated parade of fantastical figures, one after another.

↑ Miyazaki shares a laugh with Toshio Suzuki at a 2013 news conference

CHAPTER SIX

VISIONS OF THE FUTURE

How and Why Miyazaki Portrays
the Possible Worlds to Come

Floating City

Moebius and the Image That Obsesses Miyazaki

Moebius's floating city *Mont Saint-Michel* (1983) distils and, for many viewers, defines an archetypal image in the visual vocabulary of science fiction and fantasy: a city that is an island in the sky, hovering serenely among cumulus clouds above the sea. Situated in the middle distance of the illustration, the sandy-coloured city presents a destination not yet attained but promising an entire civilization in its oddly traditional-looking town-on-a-hill – complete with a tower with a high spire and levels of houses and trees piled high. Our viewpoint is shared with two robed figures on a green tussock in the foreground, one gesturing at the sight, which melds the historically ordinary (in its resemblance to a common European configuration of tower and dwellings) and the otherworldly (an entire city, imperturbably resistant to gravity, almost more like a satellite in space).

It's not the first such entry in the iconography of airborne islands: Swift's *Gulliver's Travels* (1726) features the floating island of Laputa, which of course supplied the name for Miyazaki's *Laputa: Castle in the Sky*, and a visual prototype is Arnold Böcklin's *Isle of the Dead* (1880), also known to Miyazaki. But Moebius – aka Jean Giraud, a French artist born a few years before Miyazaki in a small town north of Paris – was an influential figure in the worlds of both manga and Miyazaki largely because of just this sort of eerie landscape. René Magritte had painted something similar in a Surrealist vein in *The Castle of the Pyrenees* (1959), featuring a medieval manor atop an obelisk that hovers above the sea, but Moebius's work, Miyazaki believed, had created 'a new way to look at the world'.[32] *Mont Saint-Michel* shares its name with the ethereal castle-like island in Normandy and appears in *Venise Céleste*, the first book published by Moebius's own publishing company, in 1984, the same year as *Nausicaä* was released.

Miyazaki says he encountered Moebius's work in 1980 through the *Arzach* stories from 1975, published in the French cult magazine *Metal Hurlant*. Manga artists in Japan could have seen Moebius's work when it appeared in a 1979 issue of *Starlog* magazine, which had begun publishing a Japanese edition. *Arzach* – all pictures, no text – follows a warrior and his flying steed, and elicited Miyazaki's admiration for the illustrator's sense of space and atmosphere, as well as his characters' noble solitude. The pterodactyl-like beast in *Arzach* and *Nausicaä*'s stand-up glider bear a definite resemblance, as do the stark landscapes in Moebius's work and the planet in *Nausicaä*, but it's *Mont Saint-Michel* that seems to rhyme repeatedly with Miyazaki's vision of the world.

Castle in the Sky presents the most immediate comparison to Moebius with its lost kingdom of Laputa in the sky, reachable by flying machines of one sort or another, and featuring both buildings and an elaborate garden. The film's opening credits are a streaming air-highway of flying islands, whizzing horizontally across the screen. For an aerophile (to coin a term) like Miyazaki, the notion of a city that flies must be a kind of apotheosis in the wonders of air travel. At one point, Miyazaki and Takahata, in fact, did a little pre-production work on the film *Little Nemo: Adventures in Slumberland* (1992) that featured Moebius as a concept artist. Though they left the project quickly, Miyazaki and Moebius later had a joint exhibition of their work in Paris in 2005; Moebius, by the way, named his daughter Nausicaä.

↥ *The Castle of the Pyrenees* (1959)
by René Magritte

↥ *Mont Saint-Michel* (1983) by Jean Giraud
(aka Moebius), a floating vision of an isle
off France

↥ Sheeta and Pazu in flight above the airborne
island kingdom Laputa in *Castle in the Sky*

Beyond the physical, *Mont Saint-Michel* also resonates with a recurring mode in Miyazaki, the sense of a parallel world apart, a self-contained cosmos with its own rules and spirits. *Castle in the Sky*, for one, harbours an entire apocalyptic history, now manifest in gardens tended by giant abandoned robots. But the sense of an island set apart recurs in assorted analogues throughout Miyazaki. The bathhouse in *Spirited Away*, when viewed in wide shots, looks like a top-heavy island, separated by a red bridge from the rest of the enchanted village Chihiro and her parents stumble into. In *Porco Rosso*, the elegant singer character Madame Gina welcomes pilots to her club in the sprawling Hotel Adriano that, viewed against the azure ocean, might as well be perched in the sky. *Howl's Moving Castle* offers another twist on the stacked mini-metropolis of *Spirited Away*, with an entire castle edifice crammed onto spindly legs. (That surprised Diana Wynne Jones, the original book's author, who had imagined something like a hovercraft.) Even the spire-bedecked castle in Miyazaki's first directorial feature, *Lupin III: The Castle of Cagliostro*, sits within a vast lake, its steeply raked walls rising from the waters as if floating on air.

To a certain extent, these structures serve a narrative purpose akin to the secret gardens and tunnels to other realms found throughout adventure literature, but contained in a single wondrous image. They also visualize the possibility of beholding and appreciating the cosmos in its whole; the dynamic action in each story (which is necessary to reach or obtain access to these set-apart edifices) still allows for a vantage point upon beauty. It's worth remembering that the contemplative gaze of Moebius's illustration owes more than a little to Japanese art, specifically *ukiyo-e* woodblock painting, and especially those landscapes with clear lines and subtly hued skies and seas, which can look serene even when depicting waves or treacherous mountaintops. The influence of *ukiyo-e* (often lyrically translated as 'pictures of the floating world') percolated through nineteenth-century European art, raising the fair question of who is influencing whom.

In the end, there is a possible personal key to the obsession at hand, and as so often, it returns us to the formative years of the Second World War. When Miyazaki's family moved house to Utsunomiya, they resided for some time on Hayao's grandfather's land. This estate featured a large and beautiful garden, waterfalls and a pond, all buzzing (in Miyazaki's memory) with creatures. It's not a stretch to envision this place recurring in Miyazaki's mind's eye, at once a refuge and a site thrumming with the emotions of war and his mother's illness, long after he had returned to live in Tokyo. Perhaps this memory is Miyazaki's floating city, by definition out of reach and yet fit for reimagining, again and again.

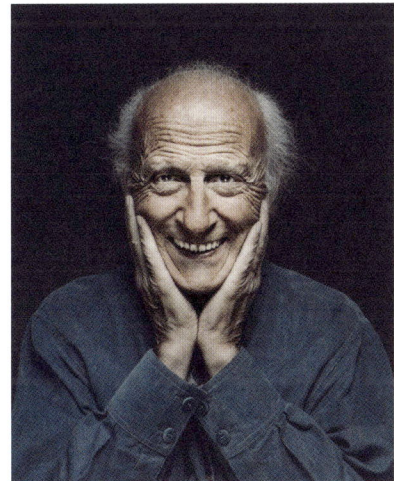

↑ Jean Giraud (aka Moebius), a mutual admirer of Miyazaki, in 2011

Apocalypse Again

Imagining Disaster
in *Nausicaä*,
Future Boy Conan
and *The Incredible Tide*

Miyazaki's experiences in the Second World War, and those of others in his generation, offer an explanation for the apocalyptic bent that continues to appear in his films. While Miyazaki himself was largely able to escape the devastation that ravaged less fortunate families during the war, it's easy to see how life after the conflict could influence his stories of survival in lands where inhabitants must start afresh. But Miyazaki's vision of a postapocalyptic future is neither hopeless nor cynical, nor rooted in the sort of fetishization of technology that courts dehumanization. That can be seen in how he adapted the series *Future Boy Conan* (1979) from Alexander Key's book *The Incredible Tide* (1970), in his first full-fledged directorial effort for Japanese television, spanning 13 hours and 26 episodes.

Key is better known as the author of *Escape to Witch Mountain* (1968), which received a well-known Disney film adaptation in 1975. His *The Incredible Tide* paints a decidedly grim picture: Conan is a castaway on an island and at 17 finds himself apparently alone in a world decimated by a nuclear holocaust. When a ship rescues him, he ends up condemned to slave labour in the city of Industria, run by a ruling group called the New Order, but he tries to carve out an existence with people he meets there. Given the freedom to adapt *The Incredible Tide* as he wished, Miyazaki immediately rebelled against the Cold War dichotomy looming within the story, whereby the New Order suggests the remnants of the Soviet Union after nuclear war with the United States.

One major step was to lean into the teenaged character of Conan, who becomes, true to Miyazaki form, a firecracker of an 11-year-old child. Born in High Harbor, an agrarian community, this Conan lives with his grandfather. Instead of the bleak, rocky landscape promised by the book, Miyazaki portrays something greener and less unforgiving and pessimistic in High Harbor, opposed to the separate caste-system state of Industria, which becomes a destination in later episodes. Miyazaki, in other words, imagines a world that might be able to recover, and a pastoral village setting that in a way anticipates the 'vaguely European' locales to which he would keep returning.

Miyazaki's softening or reworking of the implicit geopolitical dynamics to *The Incredible Tide* reflects a tendency towards unpredictable narrative that reverberates throughout his later features. In *Future Boy Conan*, he portrays characters individualistic enough to be unpredictable, whether it's the strong-willed Conan or Lana, the mysterious girl who washes up on shore, or another boy introduced (in the episode titled 'The First Friend') named Jimsy.

Later, in his features, Miyazaki tends to create triads of characters or groups with distinct motivations, rather than a singular hero struggling against an enemy and the dualities that entails. Nausicaä, for example, reckons with not only the militaristic Torumekia empire but also the initially inscrutable Ohmu beasts (as well as the festering legacies of the past). The tendency introduces ambiguous characters who can't entirely be slotted according to oppositional forces, but rather follow their own agendas. Witness Dola and her air crew in *Laputa: Castle in the Sky*, who at first appear to be treasure-hunters but later form a boisterous alliance against the nefarious Muska (who in turn end up grappling with the fascist army under their control). Princess Mononoke and Lady Eboshi are two more such ambiguous characters that create the impression of a world with several centres of power and motives that can't be easily predicted.

↑   In the post-apocalyptic series *Future Boy Conan*,
     the youthful Miyazaki hero of the title tangles with
     the dystopian state of Industria (top & bottom)

⬆ The heroine of *Nausicaä of the Valley of the Wind* in her garden lab, studying the world's complexity beyond good/bad dichotomies

⬆ The soldiers of Industria prove to be a relentless foe during the adventures of *Future Boy Conan*

Another relevant aspect of *The Incredible Tide* that drew in Miyazaki is the notion of a younger generation starting over after the (quite spectacular) failure of their elders. Miyazaki's generative faith in children lead him towards making Conan even younger than in the book, and his animation shows his trust in the untrammelled energies (and innocence) of youth from the very first minutes of rampaging around the island in *Future Boy Conan*.

Inevitably Miyazaki infuses the adventures with a suitable number of flying machines (one resembling a spy plane, others more fanciful) and robots, but despite the unlimited potential that the animated space allows, Conan's efforts are not hitched to a will-to-power obsession with technology. The promise of a new generation will not rest in the technology that destroyed the world; Miyazaki's consistent interest in machinery and gadgetry will develop differently than the prevailing *mecha* preoccupations with fighting robots that he himself decried as anime only increased in popularity. 'I like vehicles and want to continue drawing them, but I have resolved not to draw them in a fashion that further feeds an infatuation with power,' he said in 1980.[33]

Future Boy Conan would anticipate some of the action adventure of *Laputa: Castle in the Sky* later on, but it was with *Nausicaä of the Valley of the Wind*, adapting Miyazaki's own sci-fi manga, that he returned to science fiction. Anime thrived on the genre, with hits such as *Gundam* (1979–80, albeit with the robotic aspect Miyazaki had little patience for) or *Space Battleship Yamato* (1974). But much as *Future Boy Conan* redirected the story away from the desolation of Alexander Key's original novel (perhaps aided by the try-try-again serial structure), *Nausicaä* wove in animist and environmental concerns that made it more than just another postapocalyptic yarn.

Not that Miyazaki didn't have influences here as well: he's proclaimed *Hothouse*, the 1962 novel by Brian Aldiss, as a classic. Aldiss imagines a future millions of years from now, when sentient plant life has taken over, leaving a pocket of humans to carry on, with a Nausicaä-like heroine named Lily-yo. Frank Herbert's *Dune* (1965) is another unavoidable touchstone; the term 'Ohmu' in *Nausicaä* echoes the Japanese pronunciation of the English word for 'worm' thereby calling back to Herbert's infamous sandworms.

Miyazaki's film is a simplified version of his manga, which he did not complete until the early 1990s, and which follows Nausicaä on an even more complicated journey than allowed by the messianic ending of the film. But the very fact that Miyazaki kept working on the manga well after the film was released suggests his dedication to a nuanced view of the future, which did not tilt either into pessimism or optimism. No apocalypse seems to be a final ending for Miyazaki, nor any film his final word. As he said of a later movie with its own disaster element, '[*Ponyo*] ends with instability and concern for the future. But that is the fate of the human race beyond the twenty-first century, a topic that can't be settled in one film.'[34]

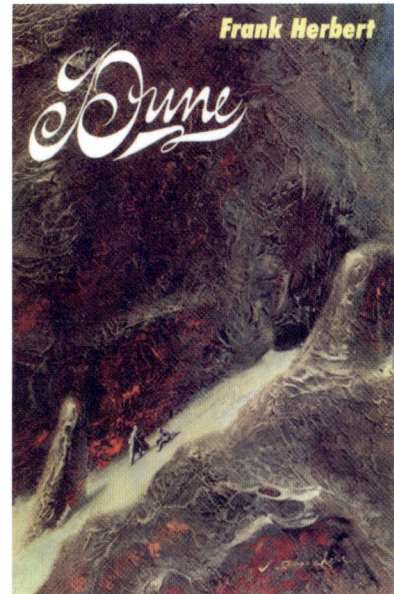

⭡ Cover of a 1965 edition of *Dune*, a prominent futuristic precursor to *Nausicaä of the Valley of the Wind*

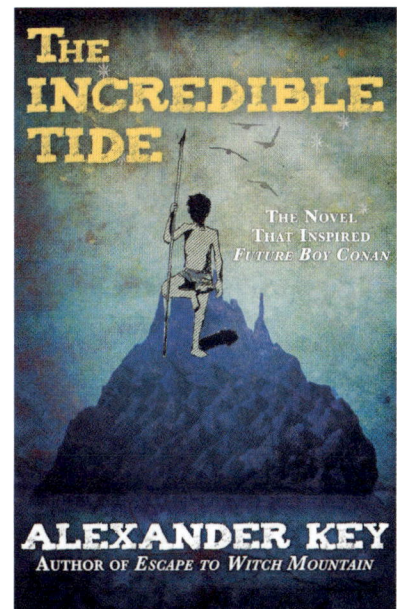

⭡ Cover of a 2014 edition of *The Incredible Tide*, which Miyazaki's *Future Boy Conan* reinvents

Miyazaki's Ecology

Making the Future Liveable

One way of predicting the future is to have an influence on it, or at least that is one way of thinking of the science of ecology, which seems to loom over Miyazaki's most popular works, like *Nausicaä of the Valley of the Wind*, *My Neighbor Totoro* and *Princess Mononoke*. Yet, perhaps contrary to the outward appearances of his films, Miyazaki can be a tricky subject when it comes to the environment, especially as it is usually discussed in relation to art. Ever faithful to the specific experiences within his films, he often seems resistant to distilling them to a general message or a critical position, as opposed to the particular positions struck by characters within the films. At the same time, his holistic view of humans and nature means that he assumes their interrelation are an integral part of reality as we know it, and thus not to be ignored. When pressed about his environmentalist leanings, for example in a 2009 onstage interview with John Lasseter, Miyazaki falls back on that very stance towards nature's changing face: 'It's just part of our natural surroundings and common sense to depict it!'[35]

In truth, Miyazaki's ethos of nature and people means that he is almost inevitably responding to the very real developments in his country. The Minamata disaster that inspired *Nausicaä* also triggered an early ecological movement oriented towards the industrial pollution that was a byproduct of Japan's rapid economic expansion when Miyazaki was a student and young animator. His own *My Neighbor Totoro*, as we've seen, inspired local conservation efforts, which in turn led to a rise in volunteer movements in Japan, as phenomena like car pollution and red tides informed citizens how everyday activities could have environmental effects. And Miyazaki, who seems to read studies of past eras in Japan as a hobby, has also cited scholarly works of ecology that track the feedback loop between human civilization and environmental change, specifically the rise of agriculture, as in Myra Shackley's *Environmental Archaeology* (1982, around when he was working on *Nausicaä*) and Clive Ponting's *A Green History of the World* (1991, as Japan's global phase of environmentalism was on the rise), which suggests that human actions can lead to societal collapse. 'Environmental archaeology' – Shackley's practice of studying organic remains at archaeological sites to trace human effects on natural surroundings – could be one way of describing *Nausicaä*'s efforts to understand the origins of the Sea of Decay and the role played by humans, past and present, in its toxic persistence.

↪
Red tide, a harmful environmental phenomenon, seen in Himeji, Hyogo, Japan, in 2007

For every vein of evidence in Miyazaki's works one can find, there are Miyazaki's protective statements of artistic intent: 'I didn't start *Nausicaä* to write a story about the ecology for the sake of environmental protection.'[36] But what's certain is that by the 1990s, the growing popular interest in ecology became a sticking point for Miyazaki that led him to see the need for a corrective of sorts to some prevalent conceptions of environmental protection and therefore nature as a force. Miyazaki grew concerned that the prevailing depiction of a planet in crisis fostered the idea of nature as powerless and weak. (One wonders if he was also

reacting to the outsized popularity of Totoro, a cute, ready-made mascot; his producer later would joke that Totoro had become a kind of enemy for Miyazaki.) Whatever the case, one impetus for *Princess Mononoke* was Miyazaki's desire to show the wildness and ferocity of nature and its flora and fauna – that 'Mother Earth' could be destructive as well as creative. For him, that was the film's most important 'message', and tellingly, contemporary to the film's release, he became concerned about whether it was communicated effectively: 'When making a film, even if it is a film for children, we mustn't tell the story without presenting its ecological issues.'[37]

And so we have the rampaging boar clan of *Princess Mononoke*, a deadly mob enraged by human incursions into the forest. Ashitaka, a warrior from the villages that suffer from the upheaval, models a kind of ambivalence opposite the tough-as-nails nature-first absolutism of Mononoke, whose face is first seen sucking blood from a wolf's wound and spitting it out. This is a far cry from Totoro and the soot sprites, but Miyazaki also includes depictions of other key players in the ecological showdown: Lady Eboshi, clear-cutting a forest to mine ore for Irontown, and Jigo, a mercenary with an unsettling cynicism about the world. Yet, in keeping with the

126

↥ An infested boar god turns demonic in *Princess Mononoke*

⇡ *The Empress Komyo* (*c*. 1820) by Ryuryukyo Shinsai,
evoking a legend about the eighth-century noblewoman
bathing a beggar who turned out to be the Buddha

complexity of Miyazaki's narratives, Eboshi is not a total villain, for she is revered as a leader by the spirited women of Irontown whom she saved from a brothel. The movie's play of motives in a fictionalized past offers a counterexample to the simplification of the real-world dynamics in present-day (or future) Japan.

Not that Miyazaki doesn't believe in the purity of nature: he has spoken often of a view of nature's sanctity as being a particularly Japanese sense of the world. As a frequent visitor to his own mountain cabin, he imbues the forest scenes of *Princess Mononoke* with a transcendent ethereality. There is also Miyazaki's own practical application of ecological practices

and environmental volunteerism, from his design of the Studio Ghibli buildings to his participation in tree-planting sorties on Hokkaido and clean-ups of a local river with neighbours. The task can seem herculean, but every individual effort has results – and has its echoes, as in *Spirited Away*'s river spirit scene, when Chihiro extracts debris from the sludge, including a bicycle, exactly as Miyazaki had in his local river cleaning group. (A mythological echo is also possible here: the story of Empress Komyo, who became a bathhouse attendant and washed a thousand people, the thousandth being a leper who reveals himself to be the Buddha Akshobhya.)

Miyazaki's ecological view of the future is therefore at once pragmatic and a bit mystical, grounded in a world of multiple tensions. Or as he phrased it once when discussing *Princess Mononoke*, which ends in both an impasse and a flickering promise of rebirth: 'Ashitaka has no choice but to suffer and live, while being torn between such conflicts. That's the only path human beings can take from now on.'[38]

The Future Is the Past

Old Forests,
the Jōmon Period and
Why Miyazaki Looked
Back to Look Forward

Quite apart from environmental concerns, Miyazaki's actual vision of the future can sound somewhat chaotic. The filmmaker has been vocal about the deleterious effects of consumer capitalism in Japan and globally, a system that he has viewed as neither sustainable nor sensible. This isn't out of an attachment to other dogmas such as Marxism, but rather because of a scepticism about or impatience with what he saw as the fundamentally arbitrary system of a civilization driven by mass consumption. He foresaw a time, even within the twenty-first century, when upheaval would put an end to the modern economy as we know it, leading perhaps to war or disease or general misery, but ultimately something better.

This isn't wholly surprising, given the tendency throughout Miyazaki's oeuvre to portray alternate versions of society, some as models, others as cautionary examples. *Kiki's Delivery Service* presents as the simple story of a young witch finding her footing in the world, but it's also a tale of mutual aid and mentoring as Kiki finds multiple female role models: her baker landlady, Ursula the laid-back artist who lives in a log cabin and the senior citizens she meets. *My Neighbor Totoro* suggests an animist utopia of sorts where humans coexist with *kami* and other spirits, while *Spirited Away* suggests the consequences of falling out of touch with such a world: Chihiro's Audi-driving parents overconfidently take advantage of the buffet, and their pig transformation evokes the dangers of unchecked consumption. It's also tempting to read No-Face, the ghostly non-verbal figure who keeps haunting Chihiro around the bathhouse, as embodying the emptiness haunting modern society, beset by waves of materialism. Miyazaki's description of the lyrical theme for No-Face sounds like an infernal vision of consumerism: 'I want, want, I so want, I want more. / Include me. / Do you need this? Do you want this? See you really want it, right?'[39]

But as *Nausicaä* amply demonstrates, science fiction for Miyazaki doesn't necessarily envision a better world in the future. The genre is not a comfortable fit for most of Miyazaki's polymorphous work, which partakes of a hard-to-reduce amalgam of Japanese belief systems, technological wonders and pure flights of fancy. As he once joked, 'in the science fiction world people talk about fourth dimension pulses and whatnot, and energy doing this or that, when the word "magic" would easily suffice'.[40] Indeed, Miyazaki is an avowed fan of the fantasy novels of Ursula K. Le Guin, whose magician saga *A Wizard of Earthsea* (1968) he claims to have read more times than he can count.

In fact, Miyazaki often saw visions for the future in Japan's past, especially its archaic past, sometimes preceding its own existence as a discrete culture. Miyazaki embraces the concept of the broadleaf evergreen forest culture espoused by Sasuke Nakao, whose work he read in the 1970s. Nakao posited that massive forests used to blanket Asia, including southwest Japan and China's Yunnan province, and that there existed a pan-Asian prehistoric culture defined by this swath of verdant nature. The region shared a number of agricultural and culinary practices in common, including apparently miso, so strongly identified with Japan. The theory appealed to Miyazaki because it suggested a community whose bonds were rooted in nature, and in fact predated Japanese identity as he had known it, which he found liberating. (It also dovetailed with his desire to see specific trees preserved such as beech or camphor, the kind so pivotally featured in *My Neighbor Totoro*.)

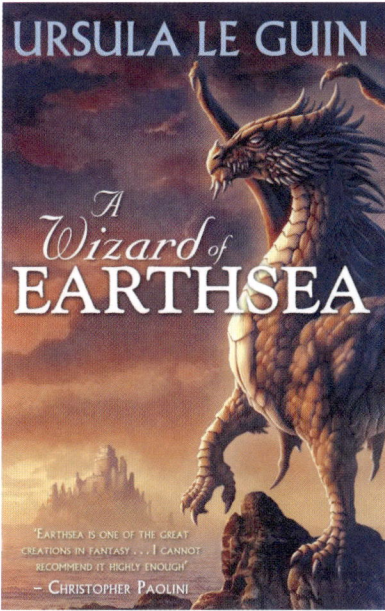

↥ Cover of a 2010 edition of *A Wizard of Earthsea* by Ursula K. Le Guin

↥ Kiki marvels at Ursula, her cool new artist friend who lives in the woods, in *Kiki's Delivery Service*

↥ Chihiro and the enigmatic No-Face ride the mystery train across the sea in *Spirited Away*

↑   Sannai-Maruyama site in Aomori, Japan, containing the ruins of a settlement from the Jōmon Period, an era that fascinated Miyazaki

↑   The complicated Lady Eboshi, leader of Irontown and mortal threat to the forest, in *Princess Mononoke*

Miyazaki was fascinated by the Jōmon Period of settlement in Japan. These neolithic people, he believed, had been wrongly characterized as essentially cavemen, when in fact they'd struck an intriguing balance between farming, hunting and gathering that apparently left them with hours of free time. An enthusiastic amateur historian, Miyazaki read extensively on this and other subjects, especially the work of Eiichi Fujimori, an archaeologist. (When Fujimori died while Miyazaki was working on *Heidi*, the animator was irritated by what he saw as the insufficient commemoration that ensued.) It must be said that Miyazaki's interest in both Fujimori and Sasuke Nakao is somewhat remarkable because these are scholarly writers with specialized interests. But the animator's willingness to plunge into the nitty-gritty of earthenware excavations is mirrored in the meticulous approach to detail and movement visible throughout his work.

For all the fantastical conceits, that work suggests a form of realism in which Miyazaki is resisting received patterns of representation to build anew from the ground up. The exact nature of Irontown in *Princess Mononoke* may be apocryphal, for example, but its warp and weft grew out of Miyazaki's curiosity about how ancient peoples must have extracted ore. To this he could freely meld more mystical beliefs, such as his hunch that trees harbor memories of hotter eras, as when he speculated about changing weather patterns in the first decade of the twenty-first century. The result is that chasing down the origins for Miyazaki's imagery can result in a cul-de-sac when it becomes apparent that what looks and feels as if it has been the basis of some actual religion (say, the deer god forest spirit in *Princess Mononoke*) or an actual form of industry (the Tatara women working bellows together with their feet, which was apparently not how it was done) has sprung from the mind of a historical and visual alchemist.

The reflexive urge to learn everything about the Jōmon Period or find other origin points for Japanese culture could sound like a conservative or, coloured by Miyazaki's anti-consumerist leanings, reactionary tendency. But as practised by Miyazaki, it feels like a form of imaginative empathy which manifests itself in characterization throughout his work. Or as he put it, when peeling back the layers on the Jōmon Period, 'It's important to avoid a fixed view of things. To not assume that people were poor here, or well-off there, or that some people are advanced while others are backwards. By opening our minds when we look at the places where we live, we can see them in a new and more open light.'[41]

↥   Clay Dogū figurine from the late Jōmon Period

CHAPTER SEVEN

DRAWN
FROM
LIFE

Miyazaki's Sources and Models
for Animating Movement

Mentor
in
Motion

What Yasuo Otsuka
Taught Miyazaki

In 2004, Studio Ghibli released a documentary called *Yasuo Ōtsuka's Joy of Motion*, a belated tribute to a giant in the medium of animation yet lesser known outside these circles than Miyazaki and Takahata. But upon Ōtsuka's death in 2021 at the age of 89, more than one obituary proclaimed him the most important figure in anime. Miyazaki revered him, giving the highest praise in the documentary when he says: 'Ōtsuka taught me everything I know about motion.' About 10 years older than Miyazaki, Otsuka had an outsized influence on his comrade as a stylistic mentor, emphasizing the very attention to lifelike movement and detail that powers Miyazaki's work, and in a career that spanned back to the early postwar days of Japanese animation.

Both a pioneer and a synthesizer of influences, Ōtsuka was largely self-taught. Coming up at a time when Japanese animation was still finding its identity, he gathered influences that included a perhaps surprising number of Western sources. At the time of postwar American occupation, that included Sunday comics read by US soldiers (such as *Dick Tracy*) and texts about American animation like *Animation* by Preston Blair, known for his work for Disney and Tex Avery. Even in Ōtsuka's childhood before then, his obsessions suggest a kindred spirit to Miyazaki: he was inspired by locomotives and later army trucks, filling sketchbooks with meticulous yet artful renderings. Ōtsuka even worked briefly for a drug-enforcement agency, where an American employee showed him how to draw and fire a gun – all more fodder for his fascination with the mechanical and inspiration from real-life sources.

Throughout his work, Ōtsuka looked to infuse the realism of his animations with the precision of anatomy and observed movement, whether it was a magical skeleton, moving bone by bone through the air, or a giant killer catfish, its twists and turns gleaned from acquiring and watching an actual catfish. While this kind of fidelity might sound second nature to animation, it was in fact a beginning of departing from 'cartoonish' unreal effects of either elastic figuration or essentially abstract silhouettes. It was as if these two animators were connected across time: one of Ōtsuka's formative jobs was working on *Hakujaden* (*Panda and the Magic Serpent*), Japan's first full-colour animated feature in 1958 – the same film Miyazaki has described as planting the seed of being an animator as a profession.

Working at Toei, Ōtsuka met Miyazaki and Takahata, at the time junior animators, but he would eventually recommend Takahata to direct *Hols: Prince of the Sun*. Ōtsuka was responsible for the harrowing opening sequence of a pack of snarling wolves relentlessly chasing and swirling around Hols on rocky terrain, images that have definite echoes in the wolf goddess Moro of *Princess Mononoke*.

↦
Poster for *Hols: Prince of the Sun* (1968), which Miyazaki worked on and Isao Takahata directed

東映
ホルスはとても強いんだ！
太陽のつるぎがきらッきらッとかがやくと
巨人モーグがあらわれる！
かわいい動物やおそろしい怪物もいっぱい！
製作■大川 博
演出■高畑 勲
☆主題歌・コロムビアレコード・朝日ソノラマ
文部省選定
映倫青少年映画審議会推薦
優秀映画鑑賞会推薦
日本PTA全国協議会推薦
厚生省中央児童福祉審議会推薦
全日本教育父母会議推薦
声の出演者
平 幹二朗
市原悦子
三島雅夫
永田靖
横森 久
横内 正
赤沢亜紗子
大方斐紗子
杉山徳子
堀 絢子
小原乃梨子
朝井ゆかり
水垣洋子
東野英治郎
太陽の王子
カラー長篇まんが
ホルスの大冒険
映倫 68424
企画■関 政次郎／相野田 悟／原 徹／斉藤 侑 脚本■深沢一夫 作画監督■大塚康生 美術■浦田又治 音楽■間宮芳生

Yet beyond the physical movement, Miyazaki in the Ghibli documentary also pays tribute to Ōtsuka's role in bringing new possibilities to animation, what Miyazaki described as 'the world of Chishū Ryū', referring to the actor who appeared in almost all of Yasujirō Ozu's films. This is an intriguing and telling claim on behalf of an animator also known for the sheer sense of fun and comedy he could bring to even villainous characters, but Miyazaki saw also his ability to convey a rich sense of life as lived. Ōtsuka had taken on Takahata to direct *Hols*, against his superiors' wishes, and Miyazaki in the field of scene design and key animation; this triumvirate continued when they followed Ōtsuka to a new company to work on the aborted version of *Pippi Longstocking* and then the short *Panda! Go Panda!* (1972).

When Miyazaki directed *Future Boy Conan*, he did so on the condition that Ōtsuka was the animation director, which came to be the case on all 26 episodes. Miyazaki continued to develop depth-of-field staging so crucial to the dynamic sense of movement. They reteamed on *Lupin III: The Castle of Cagliostro* in the same roles at a different company, Telecom Animation Film. Together the two could nerd out on making machines move – think of the perpetual motion of the car chases in *Lupin*. But Ōtsuka also brought experiments in frame rate modulation – the number of drawings per second – to heighten the drama or speed of an action, leading to an impressionistic view of action that is, put simply, more exciting.

136

↥ When an earthquake hits, the passengers on the train Jiro is riding must evacuate in *The Wind Rises*, in the backstory to his rendezvous with Naoko

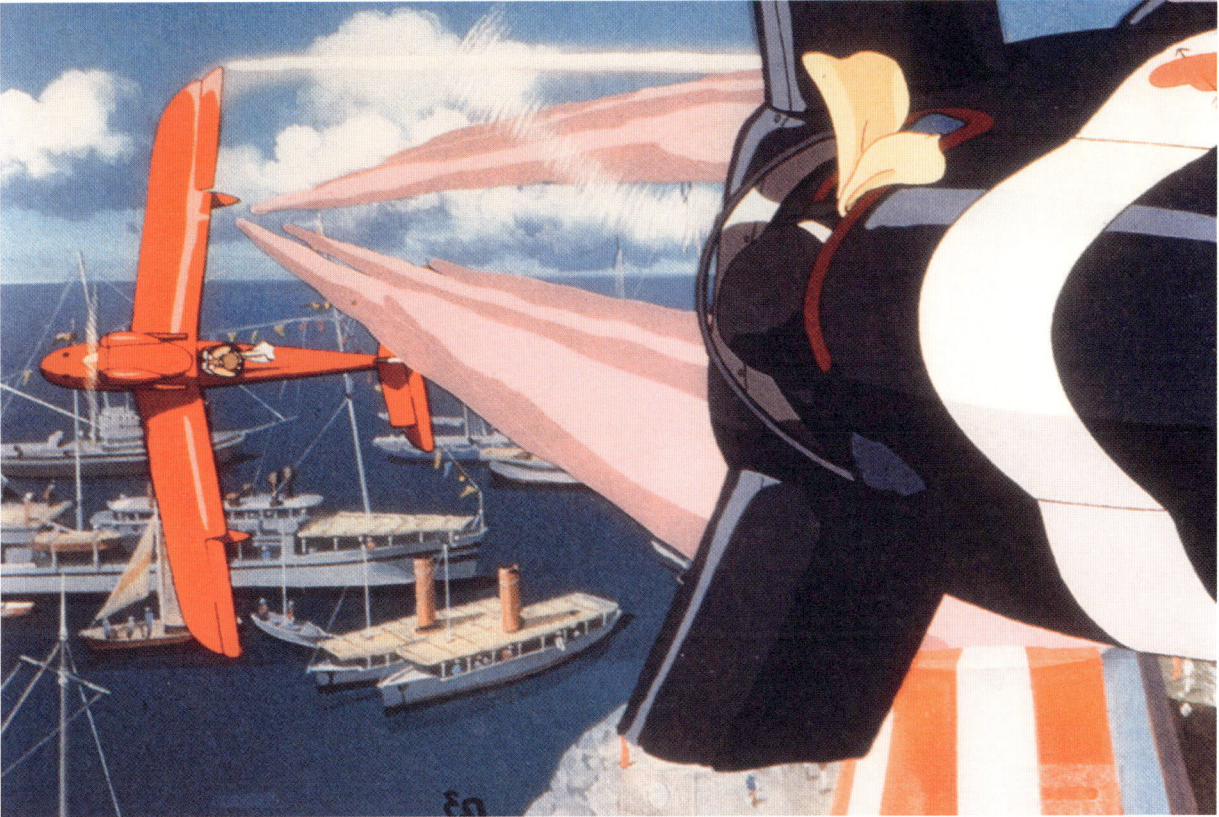

↕ The dogfights in *Porco Rosso* show off
the energizing dynamism of movement
in Miyazaki's work

In a 1980 article for *Animation Monthly*, Miyazaki distinguished between flexible perspectives of motion and what he termed the 'plastic model perspective'. By the latter phrase he meant action viewed from a fixed point, as if playing with a plastic model, versus the moving perspectives inspired by the view from the moving vehicle itself. Not that this was a dig at models: Ōtsuka, in fact, worked as an adviser for the model company Tamiya, and for a period in the early 1970s wrote a column for *Hobby Japan* about military vehicles (as he later invited Miyazaki to do for *Model Graphix* in the 1980s). It's a matter of building out from real-world

perspectives to achieve a new dynamism, perhaps even beyond Ōtsuka's work. Or as Miyazaki put it, 'vehicles are not just things with a specific form or shape, but also things we ride in to gain a moving perspective'.[42] (Miyazaki being Miyazaki, however, the article begins by quoting André Malraux's fictional description of a peasant during the Spanish Civil War struggling to recognize his land from the aerial viewpoint of a Republican bomber.)

Ōtsuka's dedication can be seen throughout Miyazaki's chases, escapes, disasters and joy rides. Miyazaki remakes rhythms and perspectives again and again, whether it's Lupin speeding

around mountainside roads to save Princess Clarisse, or Porco Rosso's dogfight with Curtis, as the camera's eye switches from stationary to mobile, at the same or different speeds as the vehicle being tracked, and from varying altitudes outside or within the cockpit or passenger compartment. The elegant trapezing of points of reference is impressive when you start tracking it, but you're always feeling it.

And Miyazaki remembered his mentor to the end. As late as *The Wind Rises*, Ōtsuka was advising Miyazaki on depicting steam locomotives, joking that his Ghibli friend only knew planes and tanks. In homage, Jiro travels on a Class 9600 steam locomotive, Ōtsuka's favourite.

Running Starts

It's the summer of 1996 at Studio Ghibli and Hayao Miyazaki isn't happy about one of the scenes in *Princess Mononoke*. He pores over one of his storyboards (or *genga*). An injured Ashitaka has rested overnight in the cave of the wolf goddess Moro, alongside San, but waking up alone in the morning, he steps outside to see Yakul, his loyal elk, waiting. Apologizing to Yakul for causing any worry, Ashitaka hops down from the cave's rocky outcropping but, landing clumsily, and a little weak, he falls over. And Miyazaki can't stand the scene, despite drawing it himself: 'Awkward, awkward, awkward,' he mutters. He reaches into his memories of falling as a child, for inspiration, then decides it's a matter of turning the character's face away from view. 'Oh, such a basic mistake! What a fool I am!' A flurry of tweaks and adjustments follow: how Ashitaka's hand hits the ground, what the patch of grass looks like and the breakdown of the actions (falling, getting up), and so on.[43]

It is half a day of work for a few seconds of screen time. Even when depicting what is inherently a clumsy gesture, Miyazaki wants the human error done right. This is by no means the most memorable of action scenes in a film with wild boar stampedes, bow-and-arrow battles and the unearthly ascendance of the forest spirit to the heavens. But the backstory demonstrates how even the smallest moments of movement and figuration on screen are informed by muscle memory, daily observation and minute decisions of animation technique that, like the source code for a computer program, are not always traceable from the final product. Miyazaki's handwringing and eureka solution might be barely discernible in the completed *Princess Mononoke*, but it's worth extrapolating this process to the natural flow of bodies through space across his many features, where secretly the most impressive animation feats involve both what's seen and what's unseen.

A strong example is Miyazaki's approach to the depiction of running, which draws on his lifelong strategy of finding variations and alternatives to established habits of animation. At times one might speak of Miyazaki's work as not so much grounded in sources as in counter-sources, or anti-inspirations, e.g. the formulae of TV series he had laboured on as a junior animator in the job of 'in betweener', creating the intermediate frames between key frames. 'The act of running in an animated film, though based necessarily on the basic form, must have innumerable variations if it is to be used to show not only what the character is doing but also what he is feeling and thinking,' Miyazaki wrote in *Animation Monthly*.[44] The variations might not be obvious, however. Miyazaki recognizes the standard way of drawing a person running: four footsteps spread across 24 frames per second, which works out to six frames per step. To convey a sprint, the temptation might be to include a picture in which both feet are off the ground, but in Miyazaki's view, this in fact dissipates the rhythm and the force of the run is not as keenly felt.

↥   The maestro sketches

⭡ *Galloping Horse*, from the Animal Locomotion
     series (1887) by Eadweard Muybridge

⭡ Ponyo runs on a wave, nimble on
     her human legs, in a virtuosic sequence

What is key is not going airborne, but rather the exertion and tension of the body when pumping the arms and pushing the legs forward. This is not how we 'actually' run, as Eadweard Muybridge so memorably demonstrated in his experiments photographing people and animals in motion: there are indeed times when both feet (or all four of a horse's hooves) are off the ground. Yet Miyazaki's focus is still on a palpable realism: movement materially centred on the body (perhaps akin to his obsession with the mechanical designs of planes and cars), not just silhouettes flung through the air. His characters may move under the skin of anime forms, and without a hyperrealist musculature, but they are grounded in a physical and gestural logic that he fastidiously relates to the often forgettable mundane reality around us. From the same essay: 'I think we must make the effort to compare the pattern against reality over and over again through incessant observation.' The approach recalls Toshio Suzuki's description of Miyazaki's memory as near-eidetic but with a creative twist: 'Naturally he can't remember everything, so he fills in the details from his imagination – in this way, the work becomes original.'

Miyazaki advises his animators to draw inspiration from watching children walking or running by the studio windows. He also regularly sets up a bench outside Studio Ghibli in order to observe the passers-by who sit there, like a live-action reference book. He'll even recruit his colleagues to act out a moment or a scene to clarify or illuminate the movement. During the production of *Princess Mononoke*, for example, he asked two assistant directors, Koji Aritomi and Hiroyuki Ito, to mime the scene in which Ashitaka carries a wounded man on his back. Miyazaki scrutinized Aritomi's hoisting Ito up, using a stopwatch to time out the beats. For Aritomi, this was déjà vu: he remembered doing the same for Miyazaki during the making of *My Neighbor Totoro*. Apparently, it was a longtime habit of Miyazaki's: co-workers on *Heidi* recall him dashing about in a car park to demonstrate a scene.

True to Miyazaki's love of the boundless energy of children, it's their running that can yield especially memorable action in his films. Consider when Mei chases Totoro with his bindle and his Totoro-ette pal at an increasingly hectic pace (after starting out by shadowing the smaller one at a walk). Miyazaki replicates the headlong and impulsive nature of a small child's run, which the child often seems only barely in full control of, and can start exactly when the thought strikes them. Mei's movement, legs stomping along, also reflects Miyazaki's philosophy of emotion through motion: she's hungry with curiosity, and it's as if she's afraid the incredible sight of two small figures will slip from not just her grasp, but also from reality.

Echoing Mei's run later in *Ponyo*, Miyazaki is even able to suggest the spirit and pell-mell pace of a child in an even wilder and more turbulent setting: when the fish-girl Ponyo strides on top of roiling waves – at one point on a giant fish's head – to keep up with Sosuke in his family's car on the embankment road. Not only Ponyo but Miyazaki himself seem to be channelling the joy of motion, and one is reminded of the animator's words in that *Animation Monthly* essay, 25 years earlier: 'Being able to show . . . running that expresses the very act of living, the pulse of life, across the screen would give me enormous delight. I dream of someday coming across a work that requires that kind of running.'

Animal Instincts

How Miyazaki Imbues His Beasts with Personality

The figure of Ponyo, and the film's marine menagerie, underlines how the animal kingdom is a font of inspiration for Hayao Miyazaki. But it's a complicated kind of influence, one that illustrates how Miyazaki's habits might be roughly divided according to a couple of tendencies. One is verisimilitude, amply clear in his attention to nuances of movement, part of a longstanding interest. At university, Miyazaki regularly went to Inokashira Park Zoo in Musashino City, Tokyo to sketch the animals, and drew both skeletal and muscular structures. But then there are his own imaginative creations in the films, which may draw upon animal habits or merge different species. These are done in a collage or magpie fashion that effectively engender a new Miyazaki mythology. And it's a habit that extends beyond animals.

What's perhaps first remarkable is the completely ordinary animals sprinkled across Miyazaki's worlds. To these beasts he gives as much attention to movement and detail as he does their human (or part-human, or spirit) counterparts. *Kiki's Delivery Service* features an intriguing array: on the one hand, there is Jeff, an elderly dog who belongs to the family of one of her clients. This St Bernard senior is fondly invested with the doddering manner of an old dog who takes his time getting around and enjoys a breath of fresh air, but nothing too exciting. He is pure dog as dog, reacting from instinct and habit. Likewise, when Kiki rides a train in a pile of hay and feels a tickle, the cows penned in the train carriage are simply responding to something new and strange in their environment with a lick. Yet a glance at the storyboards for the film reveals that Miyazaki sketched studies of cow heads from multiple angles, cocked in different poses, imbuing them with a naturalism that rivals the detail in the anime visages of Kiki.

Even in the spiritually charged world of *Princess Mononoke*, Ashitaka's steed, Yakul, resembles an ordinary red elk, and acts with a patience and caution one might associate with a tamed beast. As with a number of Miyazaki beasts, the animator also stays faithful to the resting face of so many animals, which is outwardly affectless (at least, to humans who expect facial expressions). Yakul's mood is readable more through moments of hesitation or keeping a distance, for example.

But further along the taxonomy of Miyazaki animals are those that offer a subdued version of the personality-driven depictions that are practically the rule in other animated features. Kiki's black cat, Jiji, is one example, exuding a certain feline sass (especially in the English-language voicing by Phil Hartman, a *Saturday Night Live* star). Yet Miyazaki takes care not to anthropomorphize Jiji's movements, staying faithful to the slinky movements (and near-theatrical startlement) of a typical cat. As much as anything, he seems to relish the beauty in the motion of Jiji's quicksilver silhouette. The hound Heen in *Howl's Moving Castle* is perhaps a similar example, to more comical effect: a basset-like Petit Basset Griffon Vendéen, trotting with the low clearance of a short dog and facial fur like an unkempt carpet brush.

↑ Elegant beast: Hanako, an Asian elephant
at the Inokashira Park Zoo in Tokyo

↑ San (aka Princess Mononoke) and
Yakul the Elk, Ashitaka's trusted steed

↑   Nausicaä's pet fox–squirrel Teto (a highlight
    among Miyazaki's menagerie) perches on
    her shoulder

↑   The frenetic flight of the parakeet tribe
    in *The Boy and the Heron*

↥ Haku in his dragon form with Chihiro in *Spirited Away*,
showing some canine resemblance

But even with fictive creatures or animal spirits, Miyazaki still channels identifiable features of this or that beast's habits. Teto, Nausicaä's fanged sidekick, looks like a fox–squirrel hybrid, and scurries on her shoulders as a squirrel might on a branch. Teto's wild streak also serves to demonstrate Nausicaä's bona fides as a patient ambassador to the planet's creatures: when the young warrior is bitten, she holds back a reaction, and soon enough has a lifelong friend. *The Boy and the Heron* offers a tricky case because of the story's transformations: the titular bird swoops with the elegance of a real-life heron, with attention paid to the different postures the wings take in flight and landing, but adopts different modes of behaviour when its goblin nature is manifest. In the same film, the parakeet tribe that Mahito encounters in the tower are somewhat anthropomorphized in their fascist organization, costumes and organized labour, yet when flushed into the real world, they hurtle towards the screen like panicked darts in a manner consistent with some in this species.

The worlds of *Princess Mononoke* and *Spirited Away* are complicated by the spirits and gods in animal form that are essential players in the dramatic struggle over the forest. Yet Miyazaki still draws on the organic innovations yielded by millions of years of evolution in the animal kingdom. Moro, goddess of the wolves, is explicitly modelled on *yama-inu* ('mountain dogs'), and for all her gravity-defying runs across mountain ridges, she sits up and lies down, paws out front, very much like the dog you might have in your living room. (Miyazaki, in fact, wanted to extend the canine habits to the body movements and actions of San herself, writing in the storyboard, 'She runs like a mountain dog.') In *Spirited Away*, Haku is a mythical creature, a sinuous dragon who might hail from the same universe as an Edo Period woodcut, but in the suspenseful scene when Chihiro is prying open its jaws to force-feed it the *dango* (dumpling) from the river spirit, the model was explicitly that of a reluctant dog being given its medicine. But Miyazaki can also apply animal characteristics in a

more loose-fitting manner: consider Aogaeru, a minor spirit who works at the bathhouse, who has a frog form and leaps a bit but otherwise stretches the resemblance. The Catbus in *My Neighbor Totoro* is similar, more of a cartoonish elaboration on the panther-like alacrity of some felines. And in a class of its own are the chicken legs on which Howl's castle ambulates (chosen, apparently, over soldiers' legs).

The spectrum from pursuing verisimilitude to borrowing selective qualities runs throughout Miyazaki's artistic practice. One might pick out similar habits in his use of clothing: the neat casualwear of Chihiro's parents in *Spirited Away* versus the borrowing of Bhutanese tribal costumes for Emishi Village, or the apparent Carnaby Street ensemble sported by Ponyo's sea-god father. And sometimes there is the artistic choice that seems to create its own rules: consider Porco Rosso, a suave pilot who exists as a pig – a suggestive choice by a resolutely independent-minded artist, considering that Miyazaki sometimes drew himself as a pig in his comics.

Speaking Volumes

How Voice Actors
Expand Miyazaki's
Cinema

A perennially underappreciated part of Miyazaki's films is the work that goes into voice acting. It's a puzzling oversight because the filmmaker is not only integrally involved in casting the Japanese voicing for his films, but has also taken a hands-on role in directing voicing sessions, on a sometimes minute level. The casting for the English-language dubbing, by contrast, has become part of the marketing roll-out for his films as released by GKIDS, which has continued and intensified the use of famous actors for many roles. But it's in the Japanese recording sessions that Miyazaki reveals that his exacting and passionate eye for nuance, as well as the unpredictable detail that will set the scene apart from convention or cliché, extends beyond the visual representation to the vocal performances.

It's possible to draw a parallel between how Miyazaki plucks details from real life and how voice actors are cast for his films. The art of voice acting begins with casting in many ways, because an actor who has a well-established knack for a certain kind of character, or whom audiences associate with such characters, starts with a lead on characterization simply through the signature sound and tone of his or her voice. In the case of *Porco Rosso*, the lead role was voiced by Shūichirō Moriyama, already a veteran voice actor who had dubbed many distinctive Western stars into Japanese: Charles Bronson, Spencer Tracy, Telly Savalas and Jean Gabin, to name a few. These span three generations of classic 'tough guy' actors with a gruff masculinity to their voices, and in the cases of Tracy and Gabin, with genuine dramatic depth and often an ennobling sense of tragedy. While Moriyama played many, many roles over the course of his career, this experience contributed to his match for the role, which the American voice actor, Michael Keaton, described as 'like a Bogart type, kind of cynical, kind of tough guy'.[45]

Although Miyazaki would regularly claim in later interviews that he did not watch film and television, he had previously sampled both Japanese and Western cinema extensively and seems to have had an extensive 'Rolodex' of acting talent in mind, part of the palette for any director. It made no difference if the character in question was a mythical beast: Totoro was played by Hitoshi Takagi, at the time a mid-to-late-career performer who had begun in *shingeki* ('new theatre'). Having already gone from Akira Kurosawa's *Throne of Blood* to Papa Moomin, Takagi excels at the non-verbal voicing of Totoro, a mixture of groans, grunts and snores. A press report at the time describes Takagi shaking his entire body and making the studio boom, in conjuring the otherworldly beastly noises from deep within.[46] In the case of *Howl's Moving Castle*, Miyazaki wanted one actress to play Sophie as an 18-year-old hatmaker and her transformed 90-year-old self, and had Chieko Higashiyama in mind. In fact, Higashiyama, a sunnily resilient veteran of Yasujirō Ozu's movies, had passed away many years earlier, but the specificity of his intent is noteworthy. The role went to singer-actress Chieko Baisho, a veteran of the long-running *Tora-san* film series.

↑ Sophie in her granny form
in *Howl's Moving Castle*

↑ Veteran actress Chieko Baisho,
cast by Miyazaki as the voice of
Sophie in *Howl's Moving Castle*

↑ Young Sophie enjoys Howl's gallant attentions
(and penchant for flight)

↑ Takuya Kimura, the voice of Howl in *Howl's Moving Castle*, and a hearthrob actor who sang in boy band SMAP

↑ Akihiro Miwa, the voice of wolf goddess Moro in *Princess Mononoke*

↑ Animator Hideaki Anno, shown here (left) with Miyazaki and singer Yumi Matsutoya, was Miyazaki's unconventional casting choice for the voice of Jiro in *The Wind Rises*

Miyazaki's casting comes from sometimes unpredictable sources. Howl, perhaps in keeping with his dashing looks, is voiced by Takuya Kimura, hearthrob actor who began in the boy band SMAP, selected with the help of producer Toshio Suzuki's daughter. Satsuki and Mei were voiced by adults, not children: Noriko Hidaka and Chika Sakamoto. They had voiced popular manga adaptations but delivered performances with personality and presence, eschewing what Miyazaki disdains as the 'aren't I cute?' stereotype of voicing for girls at the time. Miyazaki has a taste for non-professionals, such as Shigesato Itoi, a copywriter who (as father of the sisters in *My Neighbor Totoro*) manages to convey a kind of measured naturalism that avoids the sort of paternal warmth that the filmmaker also regarded as an audio cliché. Another counterintuitive choice was a modern legend of anime, Hideaki Anno, director of the *Evangelion* series, who had also worked on short films for the Ghibli Museum. Miyazaki handpicked Anno to play Jiro Horikoshi in *The Wind Rises*, in what became an understated, highly interiorized performance of a cerebral engineer.

Miyazaki's contributions to the direction of voice actors are emotionally precise. Take, for example, the wolf and boar gods in *Princess Mononoke*. Moro, the wolf goddess, is voiced by Akihiro Miwa, a singer and drag performer who is Miyazaki's contemporary and a survivor of the American atomic bomb attack on Nagasaki. Miyazaki encouraged Miwa to bring out both the brutality and the maternal streak within Moro, a genuinely unnerving figure on the screen, and Miwa's interpretation of Moro's laughter is richly vivid, hitting notes one might not expect. In his direction, Miyazaki points out relationships or backstories that might assist the performer, colouring in relatable emotional bonds and tensions. For Moro's encounter with the boar god, Okkoto, he suggested that the two were in fact lovers a hundred years ago, lending a certain familiar quaver to a certain line; at other points, he might suggest underplaying a moment, as when Moro confronts Ashitaka. Okkoto is a differently evocative piece of casting: Hisaya Morishige, an NHK announcer and actor whom Miyazaki listened to on a regular basis. In directing Morishige, the filmmaker referenced *King Lear* to help evoke the grand tragic struggle of the aged boar god.

Miyazaki's creative use of voicing extends to the unusual sound effects in *The Wind Rises*, which are created through human voices. Everything from the opening earthquake rumbling to aeroplanes revving to locomotives are done through vocalization, to both eerie and oddly soulful effect (with a touch of enchantment). Once again, the decision has idiosyncratic origins: Miyazaki initially wanted to do all the voicing effects himself. That helps confirm how personal the voicing of his films is to his artistic process, which the casting of the boar god supports: Morishige had voiced Xu Xian in *Hakujaden* (*Panda and the Magic Serpent*, 1958) – the movie that the filmmaker credits with inspiring him to embark on a career in animation.

CHAPTER EIGHT

DRAWN IN

The Animated Films
That Inspired Miyazaki

First Love

When Hayao Miyazaki began his career in animation in 1963, it had been only five years since Japan's first colour theatrical feature. Before the release of *Hakujaden* (aka *Panda and the Magic Serpent*, aka *Tale of the White Serpent*), Miyazaki had been interested in manga and, like others, had waited with anticipation for the latest Soviet or Disney animation to arrive in cinemas. At the same time, Western cartoons like *Popeye*, *Superman* and *Betty Boop* were hitting television, as well as a longer Fleischer work, *Gulliver's Travels* (1939), becoming available. But seeing *Hakujaden* (1958) at the age of 17 in his final year of high school flipped a switch for the young artist, whose first encounter with the film was in a third-run cinema in a down-at-heel part of Tokyo. It was a break from studying for college entrance exams, which had him drawing nihilistic *gekiga* manga as a distraction from his anxieties. Although depicting a traditional tale – the Tang Dynasty folktale 'Legend of the White Snake' – *Hakujaden* was a 'culture shock' that induced an epiphany. 'I realized that I should depict the honesty and goodness of children in my work,' Miyazaki remembers, and focus on conveying the idea, 'Become independent from your parents.'[47]

Even a casual viewer of Miyazaki's films will recognize this core sentiment that underlies the narratives for their courageous yet vulnerable young protagonists. It's worth unpacking *Hakujaden* to see what might have gripped a teenage Miyazaki so thoroughly. The Toei production opens with an overture of stylized still illustrations, narrated in song, that set up the backstory: a boy, Xu Xian, buys a white snake in a cage from the market, out of a sense of sympathy more than anything else, but adults force him to release his new companion. The animation proper then begins, with Xu Xian now a young man living with two pandas, one red. He falls in love with a beautiful, mysterious woman, Bai Niang, to whom he is introduced by her maidservant, Xiao Chin, a fish spirit. Bai Niang (who is what Miyazaki called a *mononoke*) lives in a lovely, enchanted house that, minus enchantment, looks dilapidated; when a dragon sculpture entwined around a column comes to life and takes flight, it ends up getting Xu Xian in trouble with the king's treasury. He is exiled, and the two young lovers are separated indefinitely.

↥   Poster for *Gulliver's Travels* (1939) directed
by American animator Dave Fleischer

↩
Animal Farm (1954) has echoes in the beasts of *Hakujaden* (1958)

There's more to the story, but at this point it's relevant to mention that Miyazaki felt an immediate attraction to Bai Niang, who is drawn as a porcelain beauty wearing a blue-trimmed white robe and a flower in her hair. He's said the character made him feel as if he was in love, a surrogate girlfriend at a time when he had none, teaching him a general lesson about the surrogates people seek for the unfulfilled portions of their lives. She's also a notably strong and resilient figure, like so many heroines to come in Miyazaki's own work, which must have been part of his attraction. Xu Xian must fend off a Buddhist monk who believes her to be a demon who would ensnare an unwitting Xu Xian. Bai Niang and the monk engage in a gently trippy aerial battle, with the monk wielding a crystal ball that flashes red. Bai Niang eventually must petition the dragon god to trade in her immortality so that she can be reunited with Xu Xian.

↩
Thuggish animals surround Xu Xian's panda friend during his exile in the city in *Hakujaden*

Miyazaki's interest in the film goes beyond the drama to its visual aspects. Director Taiji Yabushita and the rest of the Toei team (which include Yasuo Ōtsuka) have an evident affection for Xu Xian's panda companions and expand the menagerie by having them meet an all-animal criminal gang in the city to which Xu Xian is exiled, complete with a duck and a thuggish pig (top-heavy like an American cartoon villain), which has drawn comparisons to the 1954 *Animal Farm* animated adaptation. The sense of movement feels a bit overly synchronized, at times like cut-outs swivelled about, but the sharp colours (especially some dramatic use of red) and local backgrounds (both architecture and landscape) can be quite evocative, especially the island temple where the monk dwells and the canal city of Xu Xian's exile. Miyazaki saw echoes with the delicacy of well-crafted children's books, but by the time he had joined Toei – where he first worked on a film called *Doggie March* (1963) – TV production had ramped up and the likes of *Hakujaden* were giving way to lower-quality, churned-out product. (Even *Hakujaden*, despite its evident roots in older Japanese visual traditions, such as the illustrated scrolls that probably inspired the monk character, also arguably tapped a Disney formula of adapting classic tales with heroes, music and sidekicks.)

↑ The lovely Bai Niang from *Hakujaden*, a Miyazaki favourite

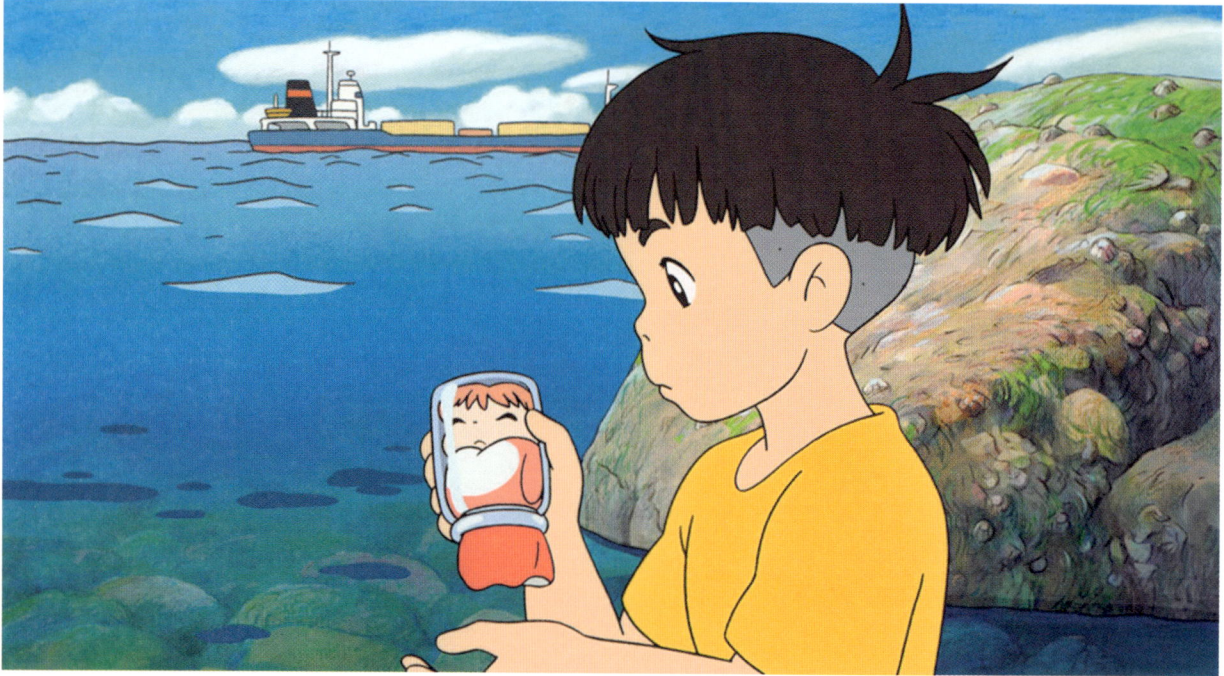

↑   Ponyo is in a jar when she is found by Sosuke,
    part of a life split between land and sea

Of course, Miyazaki too had drawn upon Hans Christian Andersen's 'The Little Mermaid' story in concocting *Ponyo*, and there are shades of Andersen's tale in Bai Niang's mutually exclusive choice between spirit and human existence for the sake of romance with a man. In fact, an extended storm sequence at the end of *Hakujaden*, featuring a monster catfish, has a similar sense of visual abandon to the sequence when Ponyo runs along the waves and on a giant fish. The waves swirl and fill the screen, and one can't help but wonder if Miyazaki was channelling his memories of this influential film. (Indeed, Xu Xian's fish-spirit maidservant, Xiao Chin, has a tender moment with friendly fish on the sea floor that echoes the world under the sea in *Ponyo*.) Other common bits of storytelling surface elsewhere in Miyazaki's work: an elongated, bucking-bronco dragon which upends the narrative for a moment (*Spirited Away*), a healing token provided by

a spirit or god (the *dango* in *Spirited Away*, versus the flower in *Hakujaden*) and maybe most significantly, in the monk who sincerely believes that Xu Xian is in danger, a third party whose motivation and actions can cut both ways. Such ambiguous characters crop up throughout Miyazaki's work – think of Lady Eboshi or the Heron - and their importance was a common theme when he would periodically bemoan about the state of anime.

But perhaps the key that *Hakujaden* holds to Miyazaki comes down to his oft-stated belief in children's hearts as a kind of true north, a sincere sentiment which he made compelling not cloying. The 1958 film after all begins with a child whose love for an animal is violently dismissed by adults, yet this love ultimately blooms into something beautiful and undeniable when he is an adult. Xu Xian embraces maturity and romance, but his open heart was there all along for any who cared to look.

↥ Xu Xian and his enchanted beloved
Bai Niang in *Hakujaden*

↥ Illustration for *Ponyo* precursor 'The Little
Mermaid' by Hans Christian Andersen:
the sea maiden saves the prince

↦
Paul Grimault,
director of what
became *The King
and the Mockingbird*
(1980), a touchstone
for Miyazaki and
his colleagues

Palace Intrigued

The Marvellous
Mechanics of Paul
Grimault's *The King
and the Mockingbird*

Hakujaden would hold a special place in Miyazaki's heart for decades, but another film released in Japan in the 1950s impressed him on an artistic level even more. That was a film directed by Paul Grimault and released in incomplete form as *The Shepherdess and the Chimney Sweep*, until Grimault was able to wrest control and finish his definitive version in 1980, known as *The King and the Mockingbird*. Even in its early form, Grimault's influence on Miyazaki's work is quite discernible on a number of levels, and was a touchstone too for his mentor, Yasuo Ōtsuka, and his longtime creative partner, Isao Takahata.

Grimault had founded a major French animation company and worked on this feature and shorts with Jacques Prévert, the eminent poet (*Paroles*) and screenwriter for films by Marcel Carné (*Children of Paradise*, *Port of Shadows*) and Jean Renoir (*The Crime of Monsieur Lange*). Begun in 1948, what became *The King and the Mockingbird* (or *The Cross-Eyed Tyrant* in Japan) adapts a Hans Christian Andersen story ('The Shepherdess and the Chimney Sweep') into a romance-against-all-odds that combines entertaining antics with anti-fascist satire well suited to Grimault and Prévert's past in agitprop theatre. In a monarchic world rendered with sharp lines and classical perspective, a pompous, cross-eyed king rules from a towering castle filled with paintings and sculptures of himself (including one riff on Picasso), all of which wealth is built upon a monochrome underground city that supplies slave labour. The shepherdess and chimney sweep are in fact figures in adjacent paintings (originally, ceramics in the Andersen tale) that hang in the king's secret apartment. When the couple escape their paintings, the king (with a dire permanent five o'clock shadow) ruthlessly mobilizes an army of flunkies and a giant robot to find and secure the shepherdess as his bride. He is flouted at every other turn by a colourful mockingbird given to speeches and clever escapes, helping the fugitive couple survive a chutes-and-ladders pursuit.

↦
The chimney sweep
and the shepherdess
enjoy a moment of
freedom in *The King
and the Mockingbird*

The high-wire action atop European architecture immediately brings to mind Miyazaki's adventure work such as *Lupin III: The Castle of Cagliostro*, in which Lupin of course interferes with a nefarious royal's attempt to marry an innocent against everyone else's better judgement. Likewise, Miyazaki's knack for developing multiple, fleshed-out settings within an adventure sees a precursor here in the king's baroquely decorated apartment, the endless architectural swoops and stairs of the palace, or even a throwaway shot of his guards' dorm room. The use of grand scale alone is noteworthy, and taken up repeatedly in Miyazaki's sweeping vistas and fantastical edifices. The aesthetic is also casually heterogeneous in the manner of Miyazaki's proto-steampunk

assemblages. The king's subjects labour in a modern mass-production factory, turning a flywheel out of sight below a trapdoor, and he keeps at his beck and call both a Vernean airship and a giant hollow-eyed robot, whom he sends in trudging pursuit of his would-be bride.

Another echo in Miyazaki's features therefore is *Laputa: Castle in the Sky*, which features its own robots on the floating sky island. In between gags and slapstick, Grimault can also find moments of strange, stark beauty, and its ending in a robot seated among ruins has an apocalyptic grandeur akin to some Miyazaki climaxes (or 'Ozymandias'). But the robot conceit must have also appealed to Miyazaki and colleagues early on, as robots were increasingly popular thanks to the manga *Gigantor*

(1963) and the demands of TV production for ever more adventure-themed output. Miyazaki was involved in the 1966 feature *Gulliver's Travels Beyond the Moon* in which an entire fleet of robots threatens a planet; *Puss in Boots* (1969), on which Miyazaki was a key animator, was Toei's homage to Grimault's film, but depoliticized into more of a comedic fairy tale. Later, as Miyazaki began to direct, there are parallels in *Future Boy Conan* between Industria and its underground tunnels, and the *Metropolis*-like ashen alleys of *The Shepherdess and the Chimney Sweeper*. Miyazaki also directed an episode of *Sherlock Hound* ('Where Did the Sovereigns Go?') about an industrialist whose castle sits atop a town, with a bird recalling Grimault's mockingbird.

↑ The vain, controlling monarch in front of two portraits that come to life in *The King and the Mockingbird*

↥ Poster for *Gulliver's Travels Beyond the Moon* (1965)

↥ Pazu and Sheeta meet a helpful robot in the ruins of Laputa in *Castle in the Sky*, an endearing contrast to Grimault's automaton

But it's important not to underplay the political bent to Grimault and Prévert's work, which can lurk beneath and sometimes at the surface of Miyazaki's, too. The French team had met in the left-wing agitprop troupe Groupe Octobre, and despite the royal palatial trappings, their film is merciless on the megalomaniac control of absolute rulers, reflected in endless depictions of the king (paintings, sculptures, even topiary) as well as in obsequious supporters many of whom dress identically. The addition of the mass production facilities and booming public address horns help connect this regime to a modern era, rather than just a fairy tale about bygone royal vanities. One is reminded of Pazu and Sheeta in *Castle in the Sky* facing off against both well-armed military forces and the hard-to-classify Muska and his agents, like some secret police who has taken the law into their own hands. Even years later, Miyazaki seems to reference the lockstep of repressive governments in the parakeet kingdom of *The Boy and the Heron*, which likewise combines fascist and royal trappings.

Miyazaki would deride the ending of *The Shepherdess and the Chimney Sweep* – the mockingbird photographing a group portrait with the titular couple in what the English voiceover calls a 'happy ending' – as typical of the silly conclusions to even good movies. But Grimault's final version, *The King and the Mockingbird*, is explicit about its priorities, namely, freedom: the final image is the robot's fist (since taken over by the good guys) smashing a cage among the rubble of the king's folly. This is political freedom, but in a sense it's also about artistic freedom. On the one hand, the king's factory is dedicated to churning out identical, ugly portraits; there's even a suited inspector peering through an observation glass to ensure there are no deviations. On the other, we have the shepherdess and the chimney sweep, who (while admittedly pretty faces with not well-drawn personalities) are literally art objects that have come alive and escaped imprisonment. Perhaps the contrast between mass production and individualism stuck in Miyazaki's mind throughout his many years of discontent working for television, until he could fashion his own brand of magic for the screen.

↦
Illustration of Gerda
from 'The Snow Queen'
by Hans Christian
Andersen, drawn by
Arthur Rackham

Pure of Heart

How *The Snow Queen* and *The Man Who Planted Trees* Gave Miyazaki Hope

The beginnings of Miyazaki's career in animation in the 1960s were not idyllic, though one wouldn't necessarily expect otherwise for a junior animator labouring away as an in-betweener. But if *Hakujaden* (*Panda and the Magic Serpent*) had been the initial boost and catalyst he needed to take the plunge into animation, before long he needed something to renew his spark of interest, and that film was *The Snow Queen* from Lev Atamanov, by any measure one of the pioneers of Soviet animation. This stark but affecting 1957 feature about a girl saving her friend from the heartless and vindictive Snow Queen's clutches was the latest of several animated features from the Soviet industry, which was experiencing a rejuvenation in the wake of the Khrushchev thaw. Miyazaki saw the film at a screening organized by the company labour union at Toei Animation, and later listened to the Russian-language soundtrack again and again. *The Snow Queen* renewed his confidence in his choice of profession and the art form generally by demonstrating that 'animation can fully hold its own with the best of what other media genres can offer'.[48]

Adapted from the Hans Christian Andersen fairy tale of the same name, *The Snow Queen* shares elements of regional folktales but also echoes of Disney and its digestion of European fairy tales. It's hard not to think of Jiminy Cricket when the pint-sized Ole Lukøje introduces the story, or even of the Evil Queen from *Snow White* when the Snow Queen appears. But the veteran animator Atamanov quickly establishes the cosy warm centre to the fairy tale that is the friendship between Gerda and Kay, children who are neighbours through a garden that bridges the windows of their homes, over an alley in the kind of traditional canted-street Western town that might appear in a Miyazaki film. When the Snow Queen kidnaps and effectively de-joys Kay after he jokes about her, Gerda embarks on a cross-country journey, a picaresque that allows scenes with a variety of intriguing female figures: a Laplander, a princess and her sibling, a bandit leader and her ruthless daughter, among others. Until they reunite, Kay coldly peers at crystals in an ice palace while the Snow Queen extols the banishment of joy, grief and love.

↦
Gerda, Kay and Granny
in the peaceful beginning
to Soviet animation
The Snow Queen (1957),
directed by Lev Atamanov

⭡ Echoes of Gerda's strong spirit can be
seen in Chihiro from *Spirited Away*

⭡ The icy duchess herself in *The Snow Queen*

Gerda seems to have left an imprint on Miyazaki with her open-hearted persistence, which reminded him of the heroine of an eleventh-century legend, 'Anchin and Kiyohime', in which Kiyohime pursues the man she loves. Gerda's mettle anticipates the bravery and tears of Chihiro in *Spirited Away* and perhaps also Kiki's many encounters with supportive women as she ventures forth on her own. The bandit leader, who hijacks Gerda's carriage, has the toothsome vigour of Dola from *Laputa: Castle in the Sky*, as well as the rough-and-tumble entourage of men. And there's an unquestionable resemblance between the reindeer which Gerda rides for part of her journey and Yakul the red elk, Ashitaka's steed in *Princess Mononoke*: they seem to have the same expression, upstanding posture and dexterous rock-leaping abilities. There might even be a flicker of Yubaba's baby from *Spirited Away* in the strange, precious princelings who take in Gerda at one point, in their luxuriant nursery room with beds that look like seed pods bursting open.

Yet any resonances might pale in importance to the specific impact of seeing this film at a vulnerable moment for Miyazaki. As with *Hakujaden*, it's not extraneous to scan the most obvious part of the narrative for how it might make a young industrious worker feel: Kay loses the poetry and love in his life – he is frozen out, so to speak, and told that this is the true nature of happiness – but then sees it all restored in reuniting with Gerda (and, plot-wise, expelling an ice shard from his soul). The sheer warmth of the sentiment and the innocence of Gerda, which is never cloying, connected with Miyazaki, and in turn these same qualities would recur in so many of the brave heroines he conceived when he moved away from serial, marketable adventures. His gushing recollection seems to support this notion of the particular glow that *The Snow Queen* provided: '[*The Snow Queen*] is proof of how much love can be invested in the act of making drawings move'.[49]

Miyazaki would compare the movement in *The Snow Queen* to that of a girls' ballet, somewhat of a mixed compliment, but its swirling ice storms have bite (they look like they'd really sting) and conjure some of the chaos that Miyazaki manages in the natural disasters across his oeuvre. (Miyazaki had an appreciation for the challenge of animating storms: he tipped his hat to Disney for *The Old Mill*, 1937, as an absolute high point for the studio in its orchestration of clouds, water and wind, even if he ultimately felt Disney amused without making him feel much.)

↑ Kiyohime, the unrequited lover from the eleventh-century legend 'Anchin and Kiyohime', came to Miyazaki's mind when he saw Gerda in *The Snow Queen*

But Miyazaki's inspirations do not necessarily have to be discerned through visual echoes in his own work. A case in point arrived much later in the animator's career (and perhaps again at a telling moment). The work of Canadian animator Frédéric Back struck a chord with Miyazaki in the 1980s, just as he was embarking on an American–Japanese co-production with Isao Takahata. The two watched Back's short *Crac* (1980), shown with Jeanne Moreau's *The Adolescent* (1979), while in the US working on *Little Nemo: Adventures in Slumberland*, from the Winsor McCay comic – a project they would be quick to exit.

Despite this false start, Miyazaki's exposure to Back's work seemed to put wind in his sails. The painstakingly pencil-drawn *Crac* follows the life of a family and area by tracking a rocking chair, from when it is first assembled out of wood by a woodcutter and gifted to his beloved, through the years it supports his wife (a mother many times over) and into its curious afterlife in an abandoned lot and then a museum. The drawings of scenes have a way of morphing into one another, giving a rough-hewn beauty to the natural scenery that appealed to Miyazaki. His interest as an amateur historian probably also meant that the humble French-Canadian agricultural community in the film, dancing and singing together, made for a fascinating example of living off the land without destroying it.

Back made *Crac*, as well as the mid-length film *The Man Who Planted Trees* (1987), later in his career, having started as a painter. And perhaps unsurprisingly, Miyazaki was a vocal fan of *The Man Who Planted Trees* as well, a film that felt simpatico to the work he was doing on the environmentally conscious *Nausicaä*. Adapting a fictional story by Jean Giono, the likewise pencil-drawn film is about a shepherd in Provence who singlehandedly revives the wilderness and communities around him by planting hundreds of oak, beech and other trees. Narrated by a visitor who tracks the shepherd across the early twentieth century, even past the Second World War, it's a heartening picture of the contributions of one conscientious man – who, we are told, lost his family – at a time when world history was showcasing the destructive drive of civilizations. Miyazaki's admiration seems to operate on a number of levels, including simply Back's skill in rendering both lush forests and the grim landscapes that precede them in way that didn't feel formulaic to him (or Takahata, an enormous Back fan): drawing fluttering leaves is, in fact, harder than it looks.

But it also reminded him of the greenery that ensued after the building of certain waterways in Japan, or the natural settings around village shrines that are left to thrive. Both forms of growth yield ways of tracking the passage of time; indeed, one piece of concept art for *My Neighbor Totoro* suggests a frame narration in which the giant camphor tree is, after many years, in the middle of a city, much like the changing surroundings witnessed by Back's rocking chair in *Crac* or the evolution of an area in *The Man Who Planted Trees*. Miyazaki even saw echoes of characters like Back's shepherd in tales he'd read from Edo-Period Japan, and perhaps felt compassion for a figure who had experienced trauma but poured his energies into creation. As *Princess Mononoke* would show, Miyazaki could be quite clear-eyed about the clashes between civilization and nature, but he was also a man who felt the old-growth forests of Japan had a cultural and spiritual centrality, and whose work, as for so many in his generation, called back to the traumas of living through twentieth-century cataclysms.

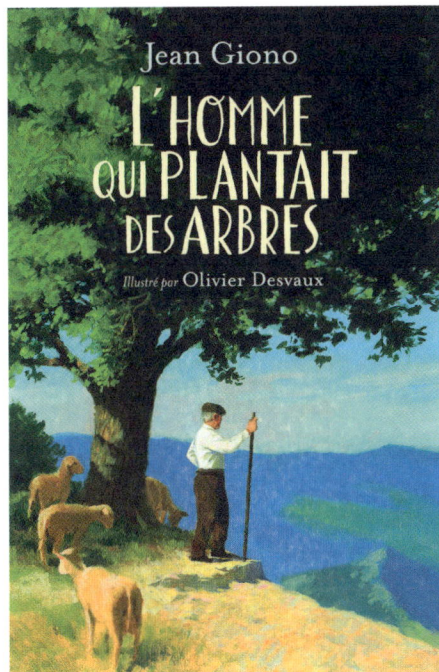

↑ Cover of *The Man Who Planted Trees* by Jean Giono

↑ Frédéric Back holds the Academy Award for Best Animated Short Film he won for *The Man Who Planted Trees*, a story of nature's rejuvenation that Miyazaki admired

↑ The heroine of *Nausicaä of the Valley of the Wind* is an adventurous student of flora

Comrade
in Anime

The Serious
Adventures of
Isao Takahata and
Hayao Miyazaki

My Neighbor Totoro has become such a classic, even an institution – Totoro's outline is the very logo for Studio Ghibli – that its exact beginnings are sometimes forgotten. The beloved film was not an immediate hit when it was released in Japan in 1988, for one thing, but how exactly it first entered the public consciousness is just as intriguing (and perhaps related to its only gradual ascent). Miyazaki's *My Neighbor Totoro* was released as part of a double bill with *Grave of the Fireflies* (1988) – Isao Takahata's sobering Second World War drama about two orphaned children struggling to stay alive after the US firebombing of Kobe. The pairing was partly a response to the view that Miyazaki's oddball *Totoro* project was an uncertain prospect at the box office. But it underlines this extraordinary pairing of titan talents at Studio Ghibli, and that an enormous influence for Miyazaki loomed under the same roof.

This influence was above all not just an artistic one, and no less important for that. Takahata had the jump-start in the industry on his future partner, beginning at Toei Animation in 1955, eight years before Miyazaki was hired. Both were involved in the company union, Takahata as vice chairman and Miyazaki as secretary, and their careers and solidarity would continue to intertwine.

Takahata, as a young director, was key to fostering Miyazaki's talents early with key positions, as well of those of Toshio Suzuki, a magazine editor before becoming the producer shepherding Miyazaki through his sometimes prolonged process in his prime. He is also attributed with recruiting Joe Hisaishi, whose scores and themes have helped define Miyazaki's films (whose characters are often described in verse in project proposals). The mutual admiration ran deep, with affectionate ribbing: Miyazaki's nickname for his Ghibli co-founder was Paku-san, supposedly for the sound of his eating his breakfast quickly (from the onomatopoeic Japanese *paku-paku*, to chomp one's mouth).

Takahata was five years older than Miyazaki, yet *Grave of the Fireflies* testifies to a strong and painful common history in the Second World War. *Grave* was based not just on the short story by Akiyuki Nosaka, but perhaps even more vividly on Takahata's own experiences of the bombing of Okayama, where he grew up. The month before Miyazaki's family saw Utsunomiya bombed, Okayama was hit with nearly a thousand tons of incendiary bombs with no warning in the early hours of the morning. Takahata woke to see his neighbourhood burning, and he could see bombs raining down from the sky; he and his sister doused themselves in water for protection. Dead bodies were everywhere – from the bombing, from drowning, from heatstroke in crowded air shelters – as they ran for cover elsewhere in the city.

↑ Miyazaki and Isao Takahata, co-founder
of Studio Ghibli and longtime comrade
in animation, discuss Takahata's film
Only Yesterday in 1990

↑ Seita holds his younger sister, Setsuko, during
the Second World War firebombing of Kobe in
Grave of the Fireflies (1988), deeply invested
with Takahata's own experience

↑ Setsuko in the haunting opening
sequence of *Grave of the Fireflies*

Takahata's memory is echoed by the opening scene of Mahito witnessing the flames and running through the roiling streets in *The Boy and the Heron*, which Miyazaki completed after Takahata's death in 2018. But Takahata had gone there first and more intensely so in *Grave of the Fireflies*, testifying to the director's investment in the most dire and frightening parts of Japanese history, with its unflinching portrayals of death: both siblings die of starvation. Miyazaki had explored dark apocalyptic fates of humanity in *Nausicaä* through modes of adventure that were his stock in trade, but Takahata's vision in *Grave of the Fireflies* provided a beacon of other kinds of realism possible in the animated genre. Indeed, the two nearly seemed to engage in a kind of creative dialogue (or two-part harmony): *Kiki's Delivery Service* and Takahata's young woman working in an office in *Only Yesterday* (1991), or *My Neighbor Totoro* and *My Neighbors the Yamadas* (1999), with its ordinary vignettes of a multigenerational family, punctuated, in Takahata's lyrical manner, with the verse of Basho. (One wonders if Takahata's university studies in French literature provided a bond with Miyazaki, a fan of Antoine de Saint-Exupéry fond of quoting other French authors.)

Miyazaki's political views are not stated explicitly in his films, though over the years he had been vocal about fears he shared with Takahata about Japan departing from the guardrails of Article 9 of its Constitution (renouncing the waging of war and maintaining of military forces). But Takahata's boldness with *Grave of the Fireflies* provided a supportive context for Miyazaki to pursue the topic of war in *Princess Mononoke*. Miyazaki was horrified by the conflicts in Yugoslavia and shocked anew by humanity's capacity for destruction; before that, it was the behaviour of the US in the First Gulf War. The fantasy world of his *Princess Mononoke* is in its way just as grisly as Takahata's historical chronicle, and while it offers the possibility of nature's renewal apart from humanity, he does not present false hope or forced alliances in the emotional détente between Ashitaka and San. It's a maturity that unmistakably connects Miyazaki and Takahata on a deep level.

Asked once to write about his colleague (or *nakama*, as he once put it in an interview), Takahata described Miyazaki as 'a man who struggles', referring to his passion and boundless energy, and love of people.[50] This is the language of a tribute, admittedly, but the sincerity feels true to their relationship when one considers what Miyazaki himself had once written in a contemplation of the future for the environment: 'The question then becomes, what is hope? . . . [H]ope involves working and struggling along with people who are important to you. In fact, I've gotten to the point where I think this is what it means to be alive.'[51]

↑ Composer Joe Hisaishi, who scores Miyazaki's films, poses with his Best Composer award at the 2009 Asian Film Awards for his work on *Ponyo*

CHAPTER NINE

LIVE-ACTION
CINEMA

How Miyazaki Thinks
Through Film History

Principles of Realism

The Dramas That
Glimmer Through
Miyazaki's Fantasies

Hayao Miyazaki entered the animation industry only a few years after Japan began making feature-length colour animations. Takahata and he repeatedly remarked on the gap between the state of Japanese animation and films like *The Snow Queen*, which they would eventually surpass. They entered a national industry that had already produced masters such as Yasujirō Ozu, Akira Kurosawa and Kenji Mizoguchi, but no such equivalents in animation. Even growing up, Miyazaki's opportunities for watching animation were not nearly as extensive as when he went to cinema with his father, an avowed movie-lover who took him to films by Ozu, Robert Bresson, Vittorio De Sica and Andrzej Wajda, as well as westerns and action films. Yet it's clear from Miyazaki's cinema that he has incorporated techniques and references held in common with live-action cinema, without losing what is particular to animation.

This applies to all the fundamentals of filmmaking, but especially light and movement, in giving a palpable sense of space to his worlds. 'I'm always aware of the light. Unless there's light, the screen won't hold viewers' interest,' Miyazaki said in an interview about *My Neighbor Totoro*.[52] The gradual setting of the sun that occurs over the course of the search for Mei serves both a narrative and emotional purpose, noting time passing by and a sense of melancholy shading into exhaustion. But even within the family's house, Miyazaki clearly determined a realistic source of the sunlight and directed the animation accordingly, aiming for a perfect sense of a Japanese summer (which, he has bemoaned, is the sort of atmospheric life-giving detail that is increasingly lost in contemporary cinema). As much as Josef von Sternberg or John Ford, and more than many of his colleagues in animation, the filmmaker paints with light. *Totoro* is also a sound example of his attention to perspective through simulating camera angles, staying at eye level for a grounded feel, with rare exceptions like the high-angle shot at the bus stop.

Miyazaki has explicitly said that Studio Ghibli aims to make films, not anime, setting the studio apart from Japanese animation he felt had lost its way from realism and shackled itself to manga aesthetics. The ethos of Miyazaki's filmmaking might also be summed up by his adherence to a multilayered plan of attack on each and every shot. 'To begin with, unless three or four meanings are behind the decision on a certain shot, a film will not have a sense of urgency,' he said in a 1998 interview about directing.[53] That's more than just a matter of his magpie research and memory, drawing on architecture, history, folklore, literature and pure daily observation of customs and behaviour, in a manner one associates more with the multiple departments of a Hollywood epic. Backgrounds in his film have a painterly detail and realistic grounding (sometimes from location scouting) that achieve the fictionalized concreteness of a meticulous film set or a repurposed location: consider the elaborate bathhouse or Yubaba's ornate apartments in *Spirited Away*.

↥ Chihiro runs 'into the camera' in a
scene set in Yubaba's apartment atop
the bathhouse in *Spirited Away*

↥ The sun breaks through the trees
in *The Boy and the Heron*, creating
a naturalistic lighting effect

↑ Drew Barrymore kisses an alien in *E.T. The Extra-Terrestrial* (1982), mentioned in promotional planning for *My Neighbor Totoro*

↑ Mei lies on Totoro's belly in the forest, to his quizzical reaction, in *My Neighbor Totoro*

All of which sets Miyazaki apart from many of his contemporaries whom he associates with manga or other anime, even as his own stated reference points in cinema can sound haphazard. In discussing how to depict running in animation, for example, he favourably recalls a scene from the 1937 samurai film *Duel at Takadanobaba*, and another from *My Darling Clementine* (1946), in which Henry Fonda takes Cathy Downs's hand to go to a dance. Yet Miyazaki's strong pictorial sense and nuanced sense of both movement and pacing might reflect a sensibility in tune with silent cinema at its peak – anything from F.W. Murnau's fever dreams to Jean Painlevé's sea creature sagas – and the classical studio output that maintained the same standards of production, whether in the US, Japan or Europe. The freedoms that animation affords to the animation then tend to add the visual and narrative conceits of particular genres.

Accordingly, *Lupin III: The Castle of Cagliostro* could partly be described as drawing on 1930s adventures from Alfred Hitchcock, such as *The Lady Vanishes* (1938) and stories of royal intrigue. But Lupin's infiltration of the castle and sense of cheek also has a streak of James Bond's feats of derring-do. The introduction to a sweet family unit in *My Neighbor Totoro*, shaded by the sadness of an absent mother, could easily be connected to the middle-class parables of love and responsibility throughout Ozu (who also had a knack for the antics of children in the likes of 1932's *I Was Born, But . . .*). The fantasy element feels native to the animation medium, which in Miyazaki's hands bestows an organic sense of Totoro and company as immanent to our world, rather than strange intruders in a photographic medium. Intriguingly, Studio Ghibli promotional plans mention *E.T. The Extra-Terrestrial* (1982) as a possible reference point, and the narrative has echoes: children, grief and a somehow comforting secret creature from another world whose odd habits we struggle to understand.

↥ Dancing in John Ford's *My Darling Clementine* (1946), one of several Hollywood movies that Miyazaki referenced in interviews over the years

The live-action reference is more explicit with *Porco Rosso*, which echoes Bogart's rough-hewn urbane hero in *Casablanca*, but again, the boundless dynamism in Miyazaki's dogfights or even the flurry of faces in the crowds below feel like effects native to animation (and perhaps illustration) rather than another cinematic source. Some have seen parallels to Steven Spielberg's *Always* (1989), though the common point of reference for these romantic adventures tinged with a tragic afterlife might be 1943's *A Guy Named Joe*. (Spielberg, for his part, is on the record as an admirer of Miyazaki's worlds and storytelling, calling *Spirited Away* one of the greatest animated films ever made.) But where to put *The Wind Rises* in the live-action family tree, when its melancholic, time-skipping melange of reality, dreams, fantasy and memory, assembling a life, conjures nothing so much as French filmmaker Alain Resnais?

That alone seems unlikely simply because of Miyazaki's avowed taste for the popular in cinema, at one point dismissing the outer limits reached by Japan's Art Theatre Guild, or foreign art-house films such as *Mother Joan of the Angels* (1961). He favoured, he said, Charlie Chaplin's *Modern Times* (1936), a choice whose mix of sweet innocence and a world in motion show evident appeal to a Miyazaki forging his own animated version of a popular cinema that doesn't lack for innovation, style and heart.

↥ *A Guy Named Joe* (1943), whose poignant romanticism around the afterlife may have inspired Miyazaki

↥ *Modern Times* (1936), the Chaplin classic that left its mark on Miyazaki and so many other artists

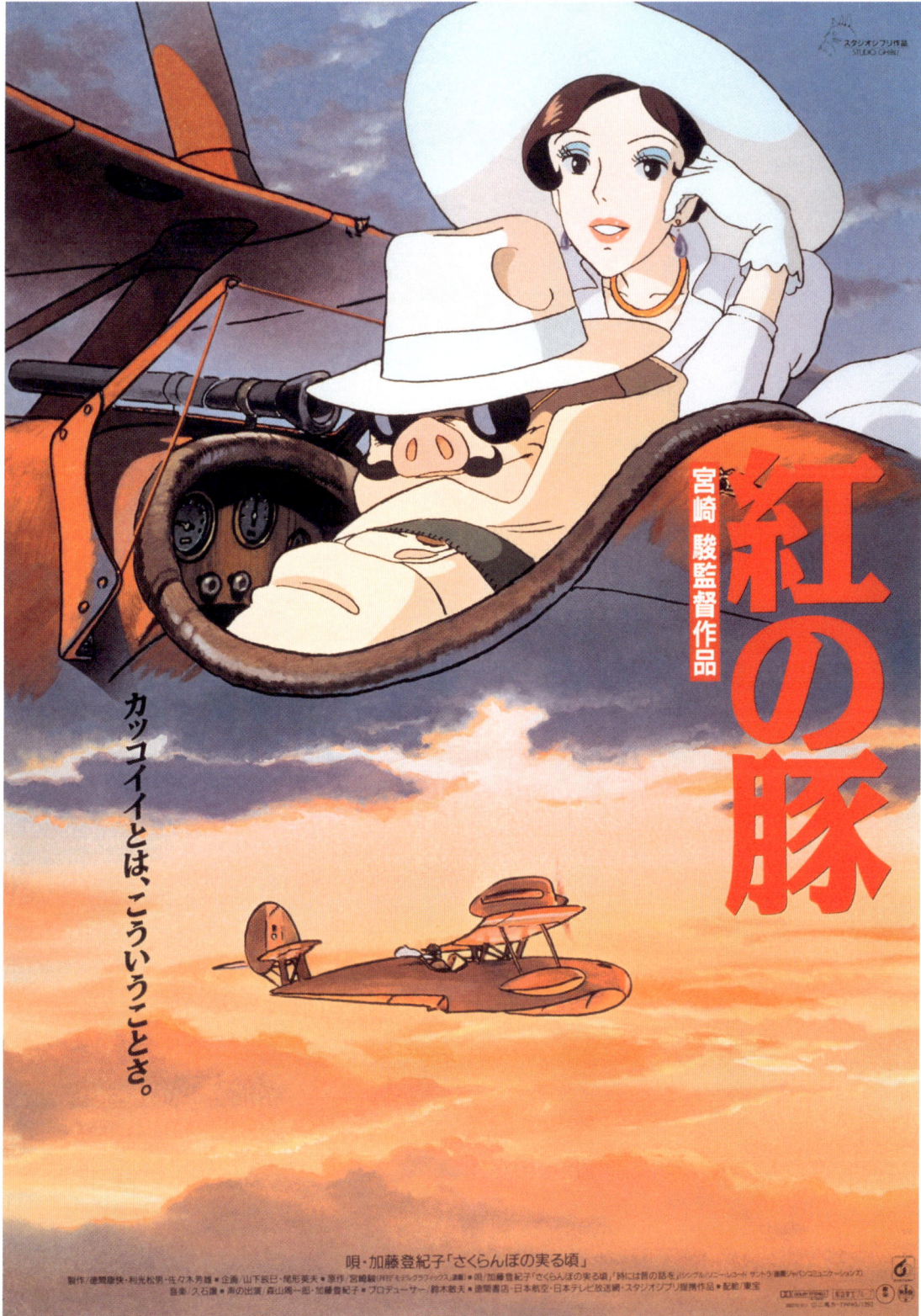

↑　Japanese poster for *Porco Rosso*

Towards a Popular Cinema

The films of Hayao Miyazaki have repeatedly broken box office records in Japan, an extraordinary accomplishment across several decades of audiences. Popular cinema is not an abstract notion for Miyazaki, who gets unparalleled freedom at Studio Ghibli but also recognizes the burden of making films that reach sufficient audiences to cover costs. But he also sees good and bad versions of popular cinema, and while he has an admiration for the entertainment value of Disney as well as the craft of particular works in their catalogue, he has also expressed disdain for the way its movies appealed to a lower common denominator, at once too broad and too low a bar. Notably, the influences in animated cinema that he has cited have largely been works from overseas, but for a model of high-quality popular cinema that both challenges and satisfies, he had a shining example right at home in Akira Kurosawa.

Kurosawa had just directed perhaps his crowning achievement in this regard, *Seven Samurai*, in 1954, when Miyazaki was still a few years from choosing animation as his vocation, much less entering the industry. But his admiration for the film's power is clear whenever he speaks of it, often describing it in terms of a magical hold: 'I too am mired in the spell of Tezuka-san for drawing and director Akira Kurosawa for filmmaking,' he said in a 1997 interview.[54] While Miyazaki grew frustrated with the creeping influence of 'Tezuka-san' (manga pioneer Osamu Tezuka) on anime, he remained an admirer of Kurosawa and, in the manner of any independent artist, paid the highest compliment of wanting to improve upon his work. *Princess Mononoke* is in many ways Miyazaki's re-envisioning of the sort of historical action epic *Seven Samurai* itself reinvented.

In telling the story of a sixteenth-century village that hires samurai to survive the incessant attacks of bandits, *Seven Samurai* features rousing, even overwhelming, action without skimping on personal dramas and vividly etched personalities. Unlike the sometimes perfunctory backdrops of its samurai predecessors, it offered a fully fleshed out portrait of a period and milieu when Japan was riven by civil wars, reaching audiences at a time when modern Japan was recovering from the Second World War. The furious battle scenes and endlessly varied camera angles on drama and action alike, often shot with multiple cameras, have both a kinetic and a concrete feel that is echoed in Miyazaki's work.

In *Princess Mononoke* and other films, Miyazaki doesn't need multiple cameras because he has animation, the equivalent of an infinite camera in imagining any frame or angle for his action scenes. When Ashitaka happens upon samurais attacking a village, Miyazaki assembles a thrilling sequence that switches up perspectives, at least a couple only available to animation. Ashitaka rides towards us, then left to right, then we are given a first-person you-are-the-camera view of the path ahead. When he shoots arrows at a samurai beating a village woman, we cut to the samurai's two severed arms still holding their sword, and then the armless samurai in a wider shot. All of which occurs in less than 15 seconds (leaving out the arrow's flight from one horse to another that decapitates another unfortunate samurai).

↥ Director Akira Kurosawa on the set of
Seven Samurai (1954), a film that Miyazaki
greatly admired as a historical action epic

↥ Battle lines in *Seven Samurai*

← The bandits attack on horseback in *Seven Samurai*

↓ Ashitaka leaps to the defence of a village under attack from samurais in *Princess Mononoke*

↥ Poster for *Rashomon* (1950), another
Kurosawa classic that left an impression
on Miyazaki

As in *Seven Samurai*, the violence
is not just thrilling, its brutality is also
felt (partly attributable, in terms of
character, to Ashitaka's curse). But
Miyazaki's admiration extended to
several other of Kurosawa's films,
as shown in a televised conversation
between the two that occurred in 1993
(then published as a book).[55] At the
time Miyazaki had a few hits under
his belt, and Kurosawa was an elder
statesman at the end of his career,
witnessing that year's release of his
final feature, *Madadayo*, about an
ageing professor. Ever detail-oriented,
Miyazaki compliments the design of
a small room in one Kurosawa scene,
which in turn brings to mind all the
memorably and vividly cluttered
meals in his own features, and notes
the gesture of putting a tea tray down,
which likewise evokes the intimate
small movements that take place in a
domestic Miyazaki scene. Miyazaki
also recalls *Rashomon* (1950) as a scary
movie from his youth for depicting the
realities of survival; at another point,
he exclaims of a beautiful riverside
sequence in *Dreams*: 'Seeing that one
scene really made me wish I had gone
into the live-action business!'[56]

↥ Poster for *Madadayo* (1993), swan song for
Kurosawa, whom Miyazaki interviewed
shortly after its release (while contemplating
a period drama for his next film)

Whoever set up the interview had apt timing: Miyazaki had been expressing a desire to make a *jidaigeki* (period drama), after the various twentieth-century settings of *Porco Rosso*, *Kiki's Delivery Service* and *My Neighbor Totoro*. It seems clear now that *Princess Mononoke* was the culmination of the desire, which his producer, Toshio Suzuki, has confirmed was partly in relation to *Seven Samurai* (and probably incorporated elements of Miyazaki's 1983 manga *Shuna's Journey*). Yet in tackling the Muromachi Period – an era which he floats to Kurosawa in their conversation – Miyazaki was intent on creating a corrective to Kurosawa's classic, which he believed had popularized an image of historical Japan as populated by samurai and peasants. Instead, *Princess Mononoke* offers not just samurais and peasants, but peasant warriors, iron workers, mercenary free agents, market folks, the unclassifiable leader Lady Eboshi and, of course, a menagerie of larger-than-life forest spirits and creatures. (Miyazaki has said he also included leprosy sufferers among Lady Eboshi's people for the same reason, inspired by a sanatorium he often walked past, Tama Zenshoen.)

Princess Mononoke, of course, contained his own historical inventions, which echo Kurosawa's own amalgams of history and imagination. And in fact some of Miyazaki's great satisfaction with Kurosawa also centred on the very real decency within the likes of *Seven Samurai* or *Ikiru* (1952), another masterwork about a Tokyo bureaucrat with a terminal disease. In the image of Takashi Shimura and all the documents his character must sign, Miyazaki saw the passage of time that no amount of dutiful accomplishments could mitigate. Not all of Miyazaki's protagonists are given the absolving stamp of well-done approval in the pursuit of their lives, whether Ashitaka or Porco Rosso, and especially not Jiro of *The Wind Rises*, whose single-minded focus on engineering coincides with the fading away of his wife.

That is the emotional realism of which Miyazaki's fantasies exist in service. Sometimes, too, the emotion can simply be wonder, as even Kurosawa recognized. As reported by his daughter, he cried at *Kiki's Delivery Service*, and in their conversation he rendered Miyazaki speechless for once: 'You know,' said the revered director of *Seven Samurai*, 'I really liked that bus in *Totoro*. Those are the kinds of things that people like me in this business can't do.'[57]

↦ A lifetime of paperwork in Kurosawa's *Ikiru* (1952), starring Takashi Shimura

↦ Jiro similarly burns the midnight oil in *The Wind Rises*, at the expense of other aspects of his life

Missing
in Action

A Consideration
of Steven Spielberg
and Miyazaki

Among modern live-action filmmakers of similar repute, the parallels between Miyazaki and another postwar director known for dynamic filmmaking seem especially notable: Steven Spielberg. The mastermind of a string of blockbusters shares with Miyazaki a total command of movement and a sensitivity to the viewpoint of children. (They both also happen to be the children of engineering types: Spielberg's a computer wizard, Miyazaki's in aircraft.) Each in his way struck a new template for what popular cinema could be and do, working in a stunning variety of settings and genre trappings: beyond *My Neighbor Totoro* and *E.T.* or *Porco Rosso* and *Always*, we might see cousins in the *Indiana Jones* series and *Laputa: Castle in the Sky* (think of the train chase above the mine) or the visually imaginative plenitude of *Jurassic Park* (1993) and *Ready Player One* (2018) with *Spirited Away*.

In fact, the galloping action and swelling excitement of Spielberg's blockbusters unleashed forces in the industry that are probably exactly what Miyazaki ended up militating against with the highly specific, becalmed likes of *My Neighbor Totoro*. But even in a film like *Kiki's Delivery Service*, which is otherwise focused on a delicate matrix of effort and care through a gallery of female characters influencing its heroine, Miyazaki lets loose with a cliffhanger action sequence featuring a dirigible, complete with a newscaster following along with the events. What might link Spielberg and Miyazaki the most is a shared influence in Akira Kurosawa and in particular *Seven Samurai*, which itself mingles action, drama and comedy.

Yet Spielberg's work can raise Miyazaki's ire in some cases, largely because of the politics of the violence in his films. That can range from the dated comic-book attitudes in *Indiana Jones*, as in the infamous gag of shooting down a swordsman in *Raiders of the Lost Ark* (1981), to what Miyazaki viewed as the video-game approach to war and bloodshed in *Saving Private Ryan* (1998), which paradoxically has also been praised for driving home the visceral terror of a rank-and-file soldier sent to combat. This is where Miyazaki's depictions of the horrors of war and his respect for the uniqueness of other beings come deeply into play as profound ideological choices. (Miyazaki also had stinging words for *Apocalypse Now*, 1979, lambasting Americans for their treatment of the Vietnam War as a matter of 'not understanding Asians', as soon as they found themselves lacking a victory to celebrate.)

In theory, Miyazaki's chosen medium could allow him to treat violence and war with a consequence-free weightlessness. But live-action films about war seem to provide another instance of a 'counter-influence' for him as we've seen earlier: the animator expressly creates harrowing depictions not intended to dazzle, but alternately to tap primal fears, or reach for the sublime, which can also be destabilizing. The opening of *The Boy and the Heron* is partly grounded in autobiographical history but soon blurs into an expressionistic waking nightmare as Mahito runs through the streets. Amid the fantastical multi-worlds of *Howl's Moving Castle*, Howl flies over a city aflame from bombs dropped by warplanes, while elsewhere a damaged battleship is glimpsed coming back from combat. This is war art meant to haunt and escape understanding, while avoiding the mechanized spectacle of live-action war movies.

↑ *Raiders of the Lost Ark* (1981), directed by Steven Spielberg – a possible Miyazaki analogue?

↑ Director fits: Spielberg on the set of *Raiders of the Lost Ark*

↑ Suggesting the adventures of Indiana Jones, this poster for *Laputa: Castle in the Sky* shows off the film's own action credentials

↑   An enchanted restaurant serves feasts to
     spirits in an ethereal sequence amid the
     bustle of *Spirited Away*

↕ Vittorio De Sica's neorealist classic, *Bicycle Thieves* (1948),
starring Lamberto Maggiorani and Enzo Staiola, one of
many films Miyazaki watched as a youth

Miyazaki has explained that one reason for an early emphasis on science fiction in animation was a kind of self-justifying industry imperative: what could animation offer to audiences that could not be done in live-action? This is why *My Neighbor Totoro*, according to Toshio Suzuki, spooked an investor, who wondered why they would bother setting an animation in everyday Japan. What sounds like business-driven bottom-line thinking turns into a glorious mandate for Studio Ghibli: create realms that meld fantasy and realism into a potent new amalgam with its own internal consistency (and not a tedious goal-driven logic that locks into place).

In fact, when it comes to one area of representation, Miyazaki is quite confident about the superiority of the Ghibli approach to anything his live-action colleagues could produce. 'The major characteristic of Studio Ghibli – not just myself – is how we depict nature. We don't subordinate the natural setting of the characters. Our way of thinking is that nature exists and human beings exist within it,' he said in a 1998 press interview at the Berlin film festival. Japanese live-action cameras, by contrast, simply 'fail' when shooting scenery, he said, joking that even their 'inept drawings' fare better. For all the splendour of a Hollywood pan across a Western desert landscape, Miyazaki's films are able to weave his characters into nature to both ethereal and haunting effect, in the same movie, with *Princess Mononoke*.

One might fairly wonder what sort of live-action realism appeals to Miyazaki, who over the course of his career has mentioned a sometimes bewildering array of films in his interviews and writings. Documentaries crop up with a certain regularity, as Miyazaki seems to be, or to have been, a regular viewer of presentations on NHK, Japan's public media outlet. (He's also been a subject: NHK produced *10 Years with Hayao Miyazaki*.) He has praised the richness and depth of a show called *Itto Rokken (One Capital and Six Surrounding Prefectures)*, and has drawn on documentary for inspiration, citing one film about child labour in Peru as an impetus for showing Chihiro working in the bathhouse rather than just visiting. (Studio Ghibli makes documentaries of its own, too, such as Isao Takahata's *The Story of Yanagawa's Canals*, 1987, and *Yasuo Ōtsuka's Joy of Motion*, 2004.)

But sprinkled among the films which Miyazaki watched as a child in his trips to the cinema with his father are not only two distinctive Japanese films, Mikio Naruse's *Repast* (1951) and Tomu Uchida's bustling single-day narrative *Twilight Saloon* (1955), but also *Bicycle Thieves* (1948) and *Shoeshine* (1946), two of Vittorio De Sica's films in the short-lived but extremely influential tradition of Italian neorealism. Known for their shooting on location in the desolation of postwar Italy, these works might seem to be strange reference points – what is 'on location' for an animation? – and yet their poignancy and lived-in daily detail make these filmmakers feel more simpatico with Miyazaki than at first blush. Decades on from these works which depicted living in a fallen world, and from the postwar portraiture of Naruse and Uchida, Miyazaki's films so often still contain the memory of disaster, and a faith in innocence striving to find a way forwards.

191

↑   Ken Uehara, Setsuko Hara and Yukiko Shimazaki in *Repast* (1951), directed by master melodramatist Mikio Naruse

Notes on Late Style

How Miyazaki Makes Every New Movie His Last

As a loose adaptation of the novel by Diana Wynne Jones, *Howl's Moving Castle* picks and chooses what to take, what to leave behind and what to alchemize into a new form for the screen. One commonly noticed touchstone for the film is *The Wizard of Oz*, on the strength of its scarecrow character, Turnip-Head, and the punningly named Witch of the Waste. Both, however, derive from the book, even if their backstories are altered and truncated somewhat, and one might better point to the *Oz*-like travelogue that Miyazaki's film provides visually, and efficiently: whereas Dorothy traversed through different kingdoms on her outlandish journeys, Howl's castle can instantly transport inhabitants to distinct realms through its magical doorway.

Yet even the wonders of *Oz* seem to provide an incomplete source for Miyazaki's film and the chaos that seethes under its neatly drawn surfaces. *Howl's Moving Castle* sees Miyazaki pushing the bounds of what his animated narratives can contain and, notably so, it introduces a phase in his career wherein his movies practically seem to be bursting at the seams. A better context for Miyazaki's renewed ambitions might be the examples set by other ageing directors feeling nothing holding them back – a late style, if you will, like that defined by Edward Said as 'what happens if art does not abdicate its rights in favour of reality'.[58] Having near-total freedom within Studio Ghibli – already a director-forward production house – Miyazaki has never had a problem with juggling reality and fantasy, but in the twenty-first century he has pushed into yet wilder realms of narrative and imaginative abundance. Where *Spirited Away* provides a roof for Miyazaki's perpetual parade, *Howl's*, *Ponyo* and *The Boy and the Heron* feel on the verge of racing and flying away for good.

For live-action filmmakers, the tensions with realism can feel particularly acute and vivid as their late ambitions grow untethered by convention and sharpen with a frankness about mortality and sometimes desire. In his final two features, Kurosawa offered a couple of examples of late style that resonate with his animator interlocutor's by turns rambunctious and contemplative later work. Kurosawa's *Dreams* (1990) summons forth a series of vignettes that draw on Japanese folklore, history, artistic preoccupations and the troubling memories that dogged the director to the end (as well as inserting eccentricities such as a cameo by Martin Scorsese as Vincent van Gogh). His final feature, *Madadayo* (1993), reins things in to portray a professor at the end of his life as his students pay tribute, in a good-humoured story inspired by the life of eclectic writer Hyakken Uchida, who survived the air raids on Tokyo to live in a small shack next to his neighbour's burnt-out ruins.

↥ Heen, Markl and Turnip-Head in *Howl's Moving Castle* summon the memory of an American classic

↥ Dorothy and the Scarecrow in *The Wizard of Oz* (1939)

⬆   The ambulating castle at rest against an
    idyllic backdrop in *Howl's Moving Castle*

⬆   *Dreams* (1990), Akira Kurosawa's penultimate
    and wondrously free-spirited film, a magical
    realist anthology film of eight vignettes

The bountiful fiction of *Dreams* gives the sense of including everything and telling all the stories one still can, as well as a return to traditional materials in its folkloric influences, rife with strange encounters with demons and mysterious personalities. *Howl's Moving Castle* features its own excess, while weaving in Miyazaki's resurgent frustrations about war, coming soon after the American invasion of Afghanistan; previously, he had protested the Iraq invasion by refusing to appear at the 2003 Academy Awards to accept for *Spirited Away*). The fantastical melodrama involving Sophie and Howl is haunted by the wars between the story's kingdoms: its opening features a parade of military forces through the streets of Sophie's city while planes stream overhead. Miyazaki does little to reconcile the clashing narratives, nor does he in *The Wind Rises*, which is retrospective and personal in its own way like *Madadayo*, catching us in a slipstream of reflections and visions that's ultimately ambivalent about work and love.

These bring to mind Said's essay on late style again: 'What of artistic lateness not as harmony and resolution, but as intransigence, difficulty, and contradiction?' *The Boy and the Heron* applies here as well, with Mahito's enigmatic fugue of dream-journeys and his trickster heron guide; the boy's path to acceptance of wartime loss is lined with such bafflement that it feels like wisdom is more a matter of survival than full understanding. The transformations and revelations in *Howl's Moving Castle* can also make for an arduous journey for the viewer, and while the ending fulfils the promise of the castle as a place of refuge – another in a series of Miyazaki's island kingdoms – the escape in a ramshackle whatzit also suggests a kind of exile.

Once again, Said is apt: 'There is an insistence in the late style not on mere ageing, but on an increasing sense of apartness and exile and anachronism.' Not that any of Miyazaki's twenty-first-century works have 'felt old' or wanting for beauty: like Hou Hsiao-hsien's ethereal final feature *The Assassin* (2015) or Kubrick's swan song *Eyes Wide Shut* (1999), itself a dream journey, Miyazaki has both refined and renewed the aesthetic foundations of his works, incorporating new digital technology (as did Éric Rohmer and other late-career filmmakers) into production. But more than ever, the perspective of age, youth and death exist side by side on a grand scale, whether *Ponyo* and its cataclysmic flood, *The Wind Rises* and its opening earthquake or *The Boy and the Heron* and its inaugural firestorms.

At this point, it might fairly be pointed out that Miyazaki's late style has extended at least since his sixties with *Howl's Moving Castle*. But oddly enough, the mercurial master has built a kind of mortality into his very method of working: every other film, it seems, he declares to be his last before retiring. (This puts a new twist on the title of a 2016 documentary about the man: *Never-Ending Man: Hayao Miyazaki* might better be called *Ever-Ending Man*.) On one level, this habit could be viewed as a lingering protest against production schedules, as if Miyazaki is still smarting from the relentless pace of TV production he endured and lambasted decades earlier. But it's also a way for Miyazaki to go out on his own terms once he has completed a new film and, perhaps most important, make every movie as if it were his last.

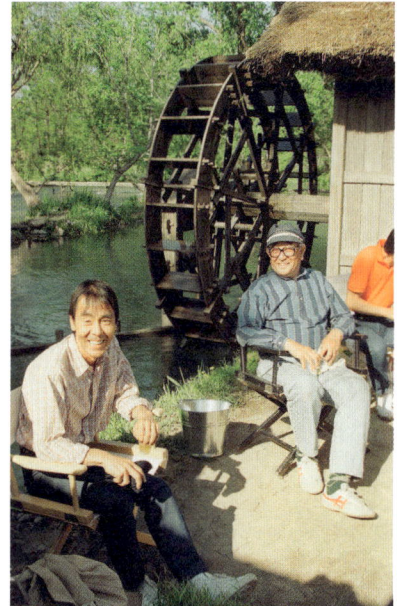

↑ Akira Kurosawa on the set of *Dreams* with actor Akira Terao

PART FOUR

CHAPTER TEN

THE
BIG
PICTURE

Four Ways of
Framing Miyazaki

Dream Logic

The Unconscious
Flow at the Heart of
Miyazaki's Stories

In *The Boy and the Heron*, the visions begin as soon as Mahito closes his eyes. He has just arrived at the house in the countryside after a long pedicab ride with his pregnant stepmother, and lying down to rest on his new bed, he falls asleep to a powerfully vivid dream. Visible through a skein of flames, his mother calls to him, then recedes and disappears. He wakes up in tears. Later, the sight of shoes at the foot of the stairs triggers a similar, fleeting flashback of his mother in flames, perhaps because he remembers running downstairs and changing shoes on the night her hospital was firebombed.

Dreams are everywhere in Miyazaki's movies, often barely signalled as a change from normal reality, and other times overshadowed by the machinations of the demons and spirits that also populate these worlds. In this the filmmaker joins a long heritage of Japanese fantasy literature and folklore, and perhaps especially works like Kenji Miyazawa's *Night on the Galactic Railroad* (published posthumously in 1934), an avowed favourite source for Miyazaki. While it's usually cited in reference to *Spirited Away* and Chihiro's train ride away from the bathhouse – and Miyazaki had wanted even more such scenes – the book is also generally a resonant narrative template for the sort of adventures in *The Boy and the Heron*, whose historical echoes exist alongside journeys unbound by time, space and logic.

In *The Boy and the Heron*, Miyazaki becomes ever more explicit about the function these fantasies serve, with their doubling of characters and obscure imperatives. The land of the dead that Mahito visits with the help of the heron is a way of working through his grief and coming to an understanding of the cycles of life and death. While there is a Buddhist aspect to this, it's also what one might describe as the work of dreams and, as such, needn't obey a rational logic so much as an emotional need. Miyazaki's inspiration comes from the experiences of a postwar generation, embracing peace but still having to process the cataclysms of war and the traumas and scars left behind. The ancient bearded figure known as the Great Uncle evokes the passing of generations, and the question of how to maintain a humane order in society that does not deteriorate.

Bringing a psychoanalytic vocabulary to Miyazaki's work isn't some incompatible imposition, as the artist refers extensively to the subconscious in discussing the creative process and how life and art intertwine. 'When I'm creating a work, I get the feeling that the general direction is always deep in my subconscious, in a place that I can't be fully aware of,' he has said.[59] Indeed, he believes he cannot complete a film without thinking with his subconscious, which takes over essentially when his back is against the wall as a creator. This might even involve 'lifting the lid', as he put it, on parts of his brain that he was not meant to expose, but for the better.

↥   *Reflection in Lake at Misaka in Kai Province*
(*c.* 1830–32), from the series Thirty-Six
Views of Mount Fuji, by Katsushika Hokusai

↥   Mahito, with bow, looks over the
horizon in *The Boy and the Heron*

↑   A 2012 edition of Kenji Miyazawa's *Night on the Galactic Railroad* (1927), a well of narrative freedom to which Miyazaki returned with *The Boy and the Heron*

↑ Caproni, Jiro's aircraft engineer guide apparition, in *The Wind Rises*, one of so many Miyazaki stories told with a dreamlike quality

The genre or mode that is the engine to this self-realization is of course fantasy, which Miyazaki views as crucial from an early age, when children have little recourse to any sort of power other than their imagination. For Miyazaki, this working-through process continues for him as an adult artist, and in one fascinating interview he seemed to come to this realization in real-time, like a patient in therapy. Talking of a moment in *My Neighbor Totoro* when Mei falls asleep while playing with a toy, Miyazaki recalls coming home from school to an empty house because his father was working and his mother was in hospital, connecting the poignancy of Mei's situation with a sick mother and the loneliness of his own childhood memory. There's a projective potency to his films that invites identification and revelation, even for the person who created them.

Dreams are even part of *The Wind Rises*, as Jiro finds the Italian aeroplane designer Caproni to be a kind of coach in his subconscious, guiding and goading him to greater heights. Rather than a convenient device to show an interior monologue, these sequences reflect that Miyazaki regards dreams as integral to the labour of a creative mind, and so any story of the creative process would have to include it (even if the figure is absent from Jiro's memoirs). It's also possible to overlay another dreamlike reading on *The Boy and the Heron*, confirmed in the documentary *Hayao Miyazaki and the Heron* (2024), that it plays out the psychodrama of Studio Ghibli – with Mahito as Miyazaki, the heron as Suzuki, and the bearded, wizardly Great Uncle as Isao Takahata, who passed away during the production of the film in 2018. A key influence on this film is not just Miyazaki's personal sense of mortality, but also the mortality of his creative home, Studio Ghibli.

Put another way, dreams are real, emotionally speaking (or as the choreographer and filmmaker Yvonne Rainer put it: 'feelings are facts'). In Miyazaki's worlds, dreams might even be real in other ways, as one is reminded by the circular exchange when Satsuki and Mei in *My Neighbor Totoro* wake up after dreaming that Totoro had cast a spell on a patch of barren land. There aren't trees in the morning, but the seeds have sprouted. As the English subtitles render it: 'It was a dream / But it wasn't a dream.' Whether or not we consider the film as filtered through a child's perspective ultimately does not matter to the child, or to us.

The documentary *10 Years with Hayao Miyazaki* features several sequences where Miyazaki talks while he works or comments on his own experience in a candid fashion. He hits upon a simple but affecting summation of what both watching and making movies can do: 'Movies show you who you are.'

World Views

A 1991 film by Peter Greenaway called *Prospero's Books* imagines the entire library of the aged magician from Shakespeare's *The Tempest* spilling out in encyclopaedic splendour in a nearly flummoxing mix. *The Wind Rises* and *The Boy and the Heron* both offer visions of plenitude, of creation and destruction, of innocence and experience, as if expressing the valedictory contemplations of a creator nearing the end of his career. In truth, this plenitude and hybridity has been central to Miyazaki's mind for decades, as he follows his passions, convictions and eye for detail, sometimes influenced by contemporary events or personal developments, but creating worlds that acquire lives of their own that can efface any such origins.

That can effectively make Miyazaki's mind a moving target, even when we profess to know its beginnings from the source. '*My Neighbor Totoro* is where my consciousness begins. It explains how my mind works,' he said in a 1993 interview.[60] And it is true that the landmark film's unique unity of Shinto belief, natural ecological awareness, childlike purity and childhood trauma would fill many of the volumes in Miyazaki's personal library of feelings and images. Miyazaki could draw on the tradition of Japanese naturalist and pioneering ecologist Minakata Kumagusu and his notion of sacred forests, while also absorbing the wisdom of postwar fantastical sources such as Ursula K. Le Guin. We see this kind of melding too in *Princess Mononoke*. Sparrowhawk in Le Guin's *Earthsea* series must accept that the Shadow he lets loose into the world is of course himself in all his flaws – a darker side that feels analogous to Ashitaka and his cursed wound. At the same time, Miyazaki complicates any dichotomy of dark and light, and evil and good, in his films' continually complex antagonists like Lady Eboshi or No-Face.

To these past sources Miyazaki has over the years continued to bring in newer ones. The legacy of children's literature remained a constant: his colleague Suzuki has described how *Howl's Moving Castle* surged to the top of his mind when Miyazaki walked in one day with the latest monthly delivery from the children's book editor at publisher Tokuma Shoten. Miyazaki's reaction to the book – 'It's great, right? A moving castle!' – would be echoed in pithiness by his child-friendly elevator pitch for *Ponyo* to two lead animators: it's a fish with a face! Yet as *Ponyo* bloomed, it took on a practically apocalyptic scope that reflects the global perspective that also kept returning to Miyazaki's mind. It's possible to view *Princess Mononoke* as Miyazaki's reaction to a resurgence in internecine conflicts: after making *My Neighbor Totoro* and *Kiki's Delivery Service*, essentially hopeful works, Miyazaki had been stunned to watch upheavals of great scale (the fall of the Soviet Union) and horrific brutality (the war in Yugoslavia), which dwarfed any futuristic, stylized apocalypse he could envision in *Nausicaä*. Even years later, in 2013, Miyazaki would still be speaking forthrightly about the wages of war when he could safely have been creating more fantasy lands: the 2013 issue of Studio Ghibli's journal *Neppu*, the year of the release of *The Wind Rises*, was a manifesto against a conservative Japanese government that was looking at revising the Article 9 peace clause in the constitution.

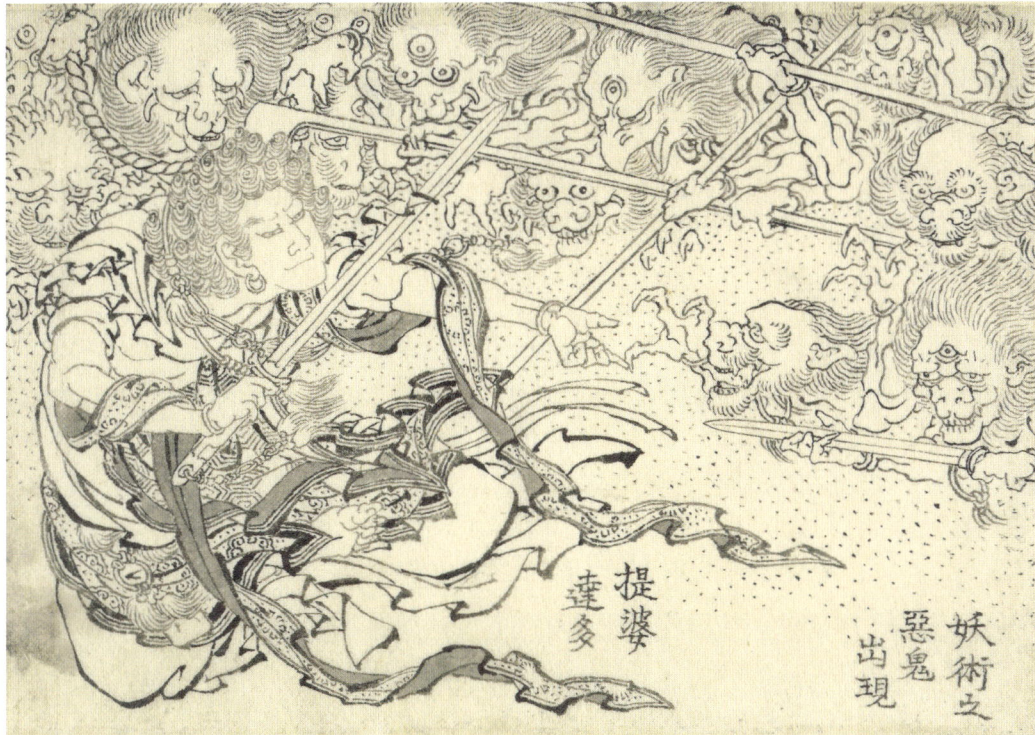

↥ *Devadatta Surrounded by Evil Spirits*
(*c.* 1820s–40s), a drawing by
Katsushika Hokusai

↥ Ashitaka grapples with a demonic curse on his arm
in *Princess Mononoke*, an emblem of a troubled realm
that Miyazaki perhaps saw reflected in our world

Not that Miyazaki believes his films can change the world, but more that they can accurately reflect the forces at work within and without us. His view on ecology incorporates an acknowledgement of the violence within nature and within people, which might explain why Miyazaki films do not turn into starkly polemic anti-war screeds. This tendency feels related to his endorsing the phrase 'transparent nihilism' by the mid-century novelist Yoshie Hotta, a prize-winning author of *Hiroba no Kodoku* and *Hojoki Shiki*.[61] This isn't the cheap nihilism that accepts the end of civilization and has done with it. Instead, describing Hotta as a kind of beacon in the ocean for when he was lost, Miyazaki seems to espouse a philosophy akin to 'recognizing the worst and hoping for the best' – and in his case, imagining the worst, as shown by his repeated, haunting visions of cataclysmic disaster and combat. Perhaps this is a Miyazakian form of ecology as concerned for both nature and human nature. Or as he humorously puts it in an interview: 'After all, Buddha worried, Confucius worried, Shinran worried, everyone worried, and we will likely continue to worry in the future. So we should all worry according to our own abilities.'[62]

Miyazaki's multiple references point to another kind of violence and upheaval that also provokes the animator's imagination. If he can be said to actively militate against anything in particular, it's the loss of cultural richness and human individuality. Every Miyazaki film is an argument and a reaction against the homogenization that we all encounter in the world. It's true to say that Miyazaki is influenced by the local lore, costumes, stories of spirits and magic, and customs of the past that distinguish Japanese culture, but perhaps it's even more true to say that the source of his fervour is a joyful preservationism that skirts convention by upending hierarchies among the disparate elements he assimilates. Often influenced by the habits and gestures of children he knows, he places his young characters in playfully amalgamated, novel worlds of past and present, in turn staving off any sense of retrenchment in the world as it is.

Perhaps this making and remaking of the world comes out of Miyazaki's heritage growing up right at the violent death of Imperial Japan, with the accompanying postwar sensitivity to any resurgent militarism, but with Miyazaki's own intense desire not to be quiet about the country's rich legacy of culture and belief. His original Studio Ghibli proposal for *Ponyo* contains an amusing diagnosis of his country (at least circa 2006), amid recommendations about how to draw eyes and what sort of lines to employ: 'Idealize present-day Japan to make it seem a bit more liveable. Raise the cultural standard of the people and get rid of overcrowded conditions.'[63] A bit more liveable, a bit more culturally aware, ever so slightly idealized – a variation on ecology we'll call Miyazaki-ology.

Welcome to the Canon

A compliment sometimes bestowed upon picturesque films is that every shot could be hung as a painting, and this certainly applies to the works of Hayao Miyazaki. Every one of his films has a particular moment of rapture, a cascading flow of action or a vista that opens up in layers. *Spirited Away* is especially rich in this regard – the spirits crossing the bridge to the bathhouse, the railway station across the water (and the train cabin) or even the playroom of Yubaba's monstrous youngster, Boh. But the moments are legion: Porco Rosso's dogfight crowds and trail of planes to heaven, Ponyo's galloping on a wave, the floating islands in *Laputa: Castle in the Sky*, the ghostly boatmen and floating *warawara* of *The Boy and the Heron*, the forest spirit transformed towering and glowing above tree cover.

In these indelible visual achievements, Miyazaki joins a long lineage of great Japanese visual artists who create their own idiom that draws on and resists tradition at the same time. Quite evidently a voracious consumer of Japanese literature, art and religion, Miyazaki fully accepts his position in this continuum (and in contradistinction to the shallower ends of the worlds of anime or manga). More than taking part, he sees this expansive tradition as being central to Japanese identity. In his acceptance speech for the Japan Cartoonists' Association Prize in 1994, he described an all-encompassing artistic ambition and faith: 'Japanese people have a long tradition of believing that they can represent all worldly phenomena with a combination of drawings and words. Politics, economics, religion, art, war, eroticism – there is nothing that narrative picture scrolls did not attempt to depict. We have inherited this tradition and continue it today.'

Though feature-length animation is a team endeavor, Miyazaki's hands-on methods display the tendencies of someone acting as if he is still just one artist at a desk. Drawing concepts in watercolour, he relishes all his habits of putting images to the page, singeing the tips of his watercolour brushes with a lighter, or choosing just the right Holbein coloured pencils. He not only drafts storyboards but also redoes the drawings of other animators if they are not to his satisfaction; he even redrew the flames of Calcifer in *Howl's Moving Castle* and individual waves in *Ponyo*. He's indeed reliant on the talents of his background animators, his colour designer – most famously the great Michiyo Yasuda – and many others. Yet his solitary creative fervour and dedication to his eclectic subjects put him in touch with traditions such as Edo Period woodblock printing, and especially in the genre of *ukiyo-e*.

For example, Miyazaki's diverse procession of spirits making their way across the bridge in *Spirited Away*, to the welcomes of bath attendants, is readily identifiable as akin to the trope of *Hyakki Yagyō* ('Night Parade of 100 Demons'). Tsukioka Yoshitoshi's 1865 version of *Hyakki Yagyō* includes at least a few gallivanting, playfully grotesque spirits who would fit right into Miyazaki's menagerie (through which Chihiro and Haku had to weave to infiltrate the bathhouse without Chihiro being recognized as human). The legendary Katsushika Hokusai also left his mark on Miyazaki as he did on so many artists: the curling, screen-filling waves and underwater views in *Ponyo* feel related to *The Great Wave Off Kanagawa* (1831) – Miyazaki has said as much – and the lesser-known *Three Turtles in Water* (1834).

↥   *The Great Wave Off Kanagawa* (*c.* 1830–32),
from the series Thirty-Six Views of Mount
Fuji, by Katsushika Hokusai

↥   Escaping the storm while Ponyo pursues, in one of
several images in Miyazaki's work that effortlessly
shares in deep traditions of Japanese art

The Hanging-Cloud Bridge at
Mount Gyôdô near Ashikaga
(c. 1833–34), from the series
Remarkable Views of Bridges
in Various Provinces, by
Katsushika Hokusai

Hokusai's portrayals of crowds also have an echo in Miyazaki's busier gatherings, as with the melange of spectators gathered to watch Porco and Curtis battle in the air. *The Hanging-Cloud Bridge* (c. 1833–34) and Hokusai's other landscapes, with mountains and clouds floating and streaming across the canvas, are another touchstone for Miyazaki's contemplative wide shots, like the railway across the water from the bathhouse in *Spirited Away*, or the same bathhouse when viewed in profile. Utagawa Kunisada also feels like a fellow traveller with his rollicking animal adventure tableaus, and a more recent artist, Kawase Hasui, is a typical comparison for the house at night in *My Neighbor Totoro*. The crowded cityscapes of *The Wind Rises* open up their own avenue of comparisons, but to all these inspirations Miyazaki's films bring another dimension with the careful processes of animation: the appearance of the deer god in *Princess Mononoke*, for example, gives its own illusion of extreme depth through the use of a multi-plane camera technique to photograph the background and the seven layers of cels (transparent sheets on which the animator draws or paints, for use in animation).

Miyazaki would probably welcome including these traditions in discussions of the films: Studio Ghibli has helped put on exhibitions rich in visual arts history. One featured Ghibli-animated portions of the *Chōjū Jinbutsu Giga* (*Scrolls of Frolicking Animals*), a twelfth-century series of inked picture scrolls that is sometimes referred to as Japan's oldest manga. Studio Ghibli also once planned out a Hokusai exhibition, which only underlines the throughline from that artist's elegant interpretations of social and natural phenomena, with attention to gestural and in-the-moment detail. Miyazaki's control of tricky perspectives and long views also owes a lot to the control of scale and line in *ukiyo-e* art generally.

Miyazaki's work itself serves as a kind of museum, or magpie-style compendium, of Japanese arts. Witness the interiors in the *Spirited Away* bathhouse, whose scenery paintings resemble those made by Araki Jippo for the Hyakudan Kaidan. Or the swords carried by Ashitaka and Kaya in *Princess Mononoke*, which belong to a special style of forged sword called *warabite-tou*, found only in the Tohoku region. Even hairstyles don't escape Miyazaki's eye: Lin, the bathhouse worker who takes Chihiro under her wing, sports a *sagekami* style that can be found in the Edo Period drawing *Women of a Public Bathhouse, Yuna*. Miyazaki also notably includes outsider art in *Kiki's Delivery Service*: Ursula's painting of a Pegasus is based upon an artwork made by children from a special-needs school. Western art, too, feeds Miyazaki's wide-ranging tastes, such as John Everett Millais's *Ophelia* (1851–52) in *Ponyo* or Arnold Böcklin's *Isle of the Dead* (1880) for the cypress grove in the cemetery in *The Boy and the Heron*.

Even the very colour selection in a Miyazaki movie embeds culture and history on a molecular level, as Yasuda was known for taking into consideration the original materials of the clothing and tools depicted in Miyazaki's animations, in putting together her colour specification guidelines. Through and through, Miyazaki's films are grounded in a greater artistic tradition even as they break new ground on their own.

↑   *Isle of the Dead* (fifth version, 1886) by Arnold Böcklin

↑   *Ophelia* (*c.* 1851–52) by John Everett Millais, a painting Miyazaki encountered firsthand and reinterpreted in *Ponyo*

君たちはどう生きるか

宮﨑 駿 監督作品

↑ Mahito approaches a mysterious gate in *The Boy and the Heron*, in a clear tribute to Böcklin's artwork

Personal Growth

How Miyazaki's
Career Is Defined by
New Beginnings

Miyazaki has made a habit of declaring retirement, only to make another film. The dramatic practice has meant that his endings always mean new beginnings. In fact, his is a career defined by beginnings, starting with his earliest years as a child during the Second World War and the trauma – and the sights and sounds – that continued to shape his films nearly 75 years later. Having frequently called the militaristic drive of his countrymen at the time a foolish endeavour (contrary to some suppositions that *The Wind Rises* reflected an indifference towards the war), Miyazaki must be sighing at the sight of the global order regressing in some ways to the brutalities of war and anti-democratic systems of government.

Sighing but probably not surprised: Miyazaki, in his films and his words, has been clear-eyed about the destructive drives that are twinned with civilization's better half. In the 1990s, he felt dismayed by his naivety that a war like that in the Balkans could happen, and then, and in the fearful months after the attacks on 11 September 2001, and the subsequent American invasions of Afghanistan and Iraq, he found himself again seeing a cycle in action. 'It made me realize that in reality nothing is really over after all. We are still in an era of great convulsions,' he said to the religion scholar Tetsuo Yamaori.[64] (Echoes from the past: perhaps Miyazaki carries on the tradition of the thirteenth-century text *Hojoki*, aka *Tale of the Ten-Foot Square Hut*, depicting disasters from earthquakes to fires and the ruins that follow.)

Also clear-eyed about a potential endpoint to current history, he continued: 'I really feel that this weird and ridiculous monstrosity, what I'd call a mass consumption civilization, has started thrashing about in its death throes.' *The Boy and the Heron* is likewise pervaded with an anxiety of what comes next, not just for Mahito on a personal level, but also for the sometimes inscrutable universal order that the white-haired Great Uncle character oversees.

The Boy and the Heron was released when Miyazaki was 82, and it's worth remembering that his own career had two beginnings. While he started in animation at Toei in 1963, he did not direct his own first feature film until 1979, when he was nearly 40, after paying his dues as an in-betweener, key animator, layout and scene designer, and so on, which might have accounted for some of his own gruff scepticism when his son, Goro, directed an adaptation of Ursula K. Le Guin's classic series *Tales from Earthsea*, despite a background essentially in landscape architecture and museum design and management. Indeed, in Miyazaki's richly imagined features, there's a sense of making the absolute most of each film's world and leaving nothing behind on the desk. The multiple retirements feel like an imperative to start from clean slates and only commit to directing a new feature if its hold on him is strong enough.

↥ *Old View of the Pontoon Bridge at Sano in Kōzuke Province* (1834), from the series Remarkable Views of Bridges in Various Provinces, by Katsushika Hokusai

↥ A frozen lake in *Evil Does Not Exist* (2023), the enigmatic eco-fable directed by Ryusuke Hamaguchi

Panda Kopanda and the Rainy-Day Circus
(1973), the follow up to *Panda! Go Panda!*,
both of which Miyazaki worked on

Not that Miyazaki's work is a solipsistic endeavour: despite some views of the perfectionist artist as ornery, he broadcasts these films from the heart, each one a new beginning. According to Toshio Suzuki, Miyazaki regards *The Boy and the Heron* as a combined act of love and a goodbye to his grandchildren, something to remember him by.[65] While bittersweet, the notion of transmission recalls Miyazaki's reaction to the first time he introduced his own two children (Goro and Keisuke) to cinema at ages five and three through the 1972 short film *Panda! Go Panda!*, which Isao Takahata directed and he wrote and served as key animator. 'For me, it was a key moment . . . *Panda! Go Panda!* is just written to describe everyday life, that sweetness that reminds us that

life can be beautiful and luminous. They watched it without moving,' he said (before noting that it wasn't successful).[66] One can imagine that this initial venture to cinema for his children would be on Miyazaki's mind when he assayed the worlds of Satsuki and Mei, Kiki and Jiji, and even Sosuke and Ponyo, whose passion for the mundane parts of everyday life (ham!) makes them doubly sweet.

For Miyazaki's audiences, too, his films provided a new beginning in the transcendent quality of their fantasy and the human detail that undergirds it, and it's not exaggerating to say that his work brought a new beginning to the perception of animation and anime generally. His films have arrived anew in a number of waves, from

the Disney distribution deal that (for all its challenges) brought the uncut Studio Ghibli films to new audiences, to the expansions of current US distributor GKIDS and new editions on DVD and Blu-Ray, all the way to unprecedented access on streaming after a crucial 2020 deal, fortuitously providing worlds to escape to during the pandemic. (Hard to believe that at one point the colourful genre studio Troma distributed the US English dub of *My Neighbor Totoro*.) This platformed progress is worth citing because it changed the nature and possibilities of Miyazaki's reception, and by now has effectively ensconced his films in the home, as the preferred cultural staple for families seeking alternatives to subpar animation and the values it often communicates.

Studio Ghibli's success might seem to make Miyazaki inevitably part of the mass consumption civilization he once decried, but the actual substance of his creative output makes no concessions to that machinery and he has spoken of working to defy fan expectations and even 'betrays' them with every new film.[67] (He's even made several shorts that can only be viewed on site at the Studio Ghibli Museum, unavailable for purchase.) Other filmmakers have recognized both Miyazaki's art and the ethos, perhaps with envy for this independence. The influence on directors and other artists has been vast, innumerably so for the field of animation (from giants like Pixar and beyond), but also among live-action filmmakers, from James Cameron and M. Night Shyamalan (who keeps a photo of his visit with Miyazaki near his desk) to Céline Sciamma and Ryusuke Hamaguchi, whose 2023 *Evil Does Not Exist* plays upon similar ambiguities and tensions around communities and the environment (as well as featuring a haunting pivotal scene of a deer beheld at a distance).

Miyazaki might even laugh at the effort to trace his sources and inspirations. 'To us, the history of modern art, the differences between East and West, or tradition versus the avant-garde, have always been irrelevant,' he once said.[68] It's more crucial for the world simply to live on, he continued, 'way beyond the left and right edges of the screen, where the sun is shining, and animal, plays and humans are alive'. Drawing on life, the worlds of Miyazaki live on.

↑   Kiki (and Jiji) about to begin the adventure of her lifetime (or simply life) in *Kiki's Delivery Service*

ENDNOTES

E N D N O T E S

216

1   Interview with Hayao Miyazaki, 'Hayao Miyazaki and Princess Mononoke and Studio Ghibli,' *Kinema Junpo*, September 1997.

2   Hayao Miyazaki interviewed by Yoko Tomizawa, *Animage*, Tokuma Shoten, 1983.

3   Interview with Hayao Miyazaki, *Roman Album: Nausicaä of the Valley of the Wind*, Tokuma Shoten, 1984.

4   Hayao Miyazaki interviewed by Junichi Takahashi and Tetsuji Yamamoto, *Kikan Iichiko*, 1994–95.

5   Hayao Miyazaki lecture delivered at Toyoko Theatre, Shibuya, Tokyo, 21 December 1982.

6   From the Studio Ghibli memo, 'Kiki – The Spirit and the Hopes of Contemporary Girls', Studio Ghibli, 1988.

7   Hayao Miyazaki, Japanese edition of *Terre des Hommes*, Shincho Bunko, 1998.

8   Hayao Miyazaki, *The Porco Rosso Memos: Directorial Memoranda*, Studio Ghibli, 1991.

9   Isao Takahata, quoted in *Maboroshi no Pippi Longstocking (The Phantom Pippi Longstocking)*, Iwanami Shoten, 2014.

10   Quoted in *Animism in Contemporary Japan* by Shoko Yoneyama, Taylor & Francis, 2018.

11   Hayao Miyazaki, Afterword to *Starting Point 1979–96*, Studio Ghibli, 1996.

12   Hayao Miyazaki speaking in the Japanese TV documentary, *10 Years with Miyazaki*, 2019.

13   Hayao Miyazaki interviewed by Takashi Yamashita, *Neppu*, Studio Ghibli, 2006.

14   Hayao Miyazaki, *Neppu*, Studio Ghibli, 2006.

15   Hayao Miyazaki in dialogue with Tadao Sato, 'Hayao Miyazaki and Princess Mononoke and Studio Ghibli', *Kinema Junpōsha*, Masonobu Shimizu, 1997.

16   Isao Takahata, Hayao Miyazaki and Yoichi Kotabe, *The Phantom Pippi Longstocking (Maboroshi no Nagagutsu-shita no Pippi)*, Iwanami Shoten, 2014.

17   Hayao Miyazaki lecture, *Films of Japan, No. 7. Nippon eiga no genzai* (*The State of Japanese Film*), Iwanami Shoten, 1988.

18   Hayao Miyazaki interviewed in *Iichiko*, Issue Nos 33–34, October–January 1994–95.

19   Hayao Miyazaki interviewed in *Roman Album: The Spirited Away*, Tokuma Shoten, 2001.

20   Hayao Miyazaki interviewed in *Roman Album: My Neighbor Totoro*, Tokuma Shoten, 1988.

21   Ibid.

22   Interview with Hayao Miyazaki, *Imperial Hotel, Tokyo* magazine, Seidosha, 2001.

23   Hayao Miyazaki lecture to Joint Animation Studies Groups at Waseda University, 5 June 1982.

24   Interview with Hayao Miyazaki, *Yomiuri Shimbun*, Yomiuri Group, 1997.

25   Interview with Hayao Miyazaki, *Animage Special: Hayao Miyazaki and Hideaki Anno*, Tokuma Shoten, June 1998.

26   Studio Ghibli, *Studio Ghibli: The Complete Works*, Kodansha Publishing, 2021.

27   Interview with Hayao Miyazaki, *YOMU (To Read)*, Iwanami Shoten, June 1994.

28   Transcript published in *Eureka*, Seidosha, 2001.

29   Hayao Miyazaki interviewed in *Roman Album: My Neighbor Totoro*, Studio Ghibli, 1988.

30   Toshio Suzuki interviewed in *Shūkan Bunshun*, 20 December 2023.

31   Hayao Miyazaki interviewed in *Roman Album: The Spirited Away*, Tokuma Shoten, 2001.

32   33 Hayao Miyazaki, *Ciné Live*, No. 86, Cyber Press Publishing, 2005.

33   Interview with Hayao Miyazaki, *Gekkan Animeshon (Animation Monthly)*, 1980.

34   Hayao Miyazaki, memo on music for Joe Hisaishi, Studio Ghibli, 2007.

35   Hayao Miyazaki interviewed by John Lasseter, Marc Davis Celebration of Animation: Hayao Miyazaki, 28 July 2009.

36   Interview with Hayao Miyazaki. *Yom.* June 1994.

37   Interview with Hayao Miyazaki, *Cine Front*, Cine Furontosha, 1997.

38   Interview with Hayao Miyazaki, Princess Mononoke Theatre Program, Studio Ghibli, 1997.

39   Hayao Miyazaki, from *Notes for the Spirited Away Image Album*, 2000.

40   Hayao Miyazaki, *Spirited Away* press conference, 25 August 2001.

41   Hayao Miyazaki, talk on the Fujimi Highland, published in *Rebirth of the Highland Jomon Kingdom: The Universality of Idojiri Culture*, Gensosha, 2004.

42   Hayao Miyazaki, *Gekkan Animeshon (Animation Monthly)*, 1980.

43   From the film *Mononoke Hime wa koushite umareta (How Mononoke Hime Was Born)*, 1997.

44   Ibid.

45   Interview in DVD supplement. *Porco Rosso*. Disney. 2005.

46   *The Art of My Neighbor Totoro*. Studio Ghibli, 2005.

47	Hayao Miyazaki, Joint Animation Studies Groups Lecture at Waseda University, 1982.
48	Hayao Miyazaki lecture, published in *Films of Japan, The State of Japanese Film* by Iwanami Shoten, 1988.
49	Ibid.
50	Isao Takahata, 'The Fireworks of Eros', *Starting Point*, Viz Media, 1996.
51	Hayao Miyazaki, 'Iki iki mizu bukku', *Asahi Original*, Asahi Shinbunsha, 1994.
52	Interview with Hayao Miyazaki, *Roman Album: My Neighbor Totoro*, Tokuma Shoten, 1988.
53	Interview with Hayao Miyazaki, *Animage Special: Hayao Miyazaki and Hideaki Anno*, Tokuma Shoten, 1998.
54	Interview with Hayao Miyazaki, *Yomiuri Shimbun*, Yomiuri Group, 1997.
55	Conversation reprinted as *Nani ga Eiga ka*, Tokuma Shoten, 1993.
56	Ibid.
57	Ibid.
58	Edward Said, 'Thoughts on Late Style', London Review of Books, 5 August 2004.
59	Hayao Miyazaki, 'Kaze no kaeru basho: Naushika kara Chihiro made no kiseki', *Rokkingu On*, 2002.
60	Hayao Miyazaki interviewed by Takashi Oshiguchi, *Animerica Anime & Manga Monthly*, Viz Media, 1993.
61	Interview with Hayao Miyazaki, *Quarterly Human Beings and Education*, Junposha, 1996.
62	Interview with Hayao Miyazaki. *Kikan: Ningen to Kyoiku*. Issue No. 10. Junposha, June 1996.
63	Hayao Miyazaki, *Ponyo Proposal*, Studio Ghibli. 2006.
64	Interview with Hayao Miyazaki, PHP Kenkyūjo, 2002.
65	Interview with Toshio Suzuki on 'Nichiyobi Bijitsukan', 2017.
66	Interview with Hayao Miyazaki in French *Vogue*, 2002.
67	Hayao Miyazaki, acceptance speech on receiving the Japan Foundation Award for 2005.
68	Ibid.

F
I
L
M
O
G
R
A
P
H
Y

A list of feature films directed by Hayao Miyazaki

Lupin III: The Castle of Cagliostro
1979
(100 min)

Nausicaä of the Valley of the Wind
1984
(116 min)

Laputa: Castle in the Sky
1986
(125 min)

My Neighbor Totoro
1988
(88 min)

Kiki's Delivery Service
1989
(102 min)

Porco Rosso
1992
(93 min)

Princess Mononoke
1997
(133 min)

Spirited Away
2001
(125 min)

Howl's Moving Castle
2004
(120 min)

Ponyo on a Cliff by the Sea
2008
(103 min)

The Wind Rises
2013
(127 min)

The Boy and the Heron
2023
(124 min)

I
N
D
E
X

AUTHOR BIO

Nicolas Rapold is a critic and film historian whose work appears in *The New York Times*, *Sight & Sound*, and *Filmmaker*, among other publications. He was editor-in-chief of *Film Comment*, interviews critics and filmmakers on the podcast The Last Thing I Saw, and has programmed film series at Lincoln Center, Museum of the Moving Image and beyond.

222

ACKNOWLEDGEMENTS

As an Ancient Egyptian text on work once put it, 'There is nothing that surpasses writing: it is like being on the water!' Or like being in the air, to borrow from the visions of Hayao Miyazaki . . . It's not often that I am able to write at length about such a wonderful body of work, much less one that's meant so much to me. For that opportunity, and for their tireless labours and surehanded stewardship, I feel grateful to John Parton and Laura Bulbeck at Quarto, Trystan Thompson at Intercity, and everyone else who worked so hard on the book. And I give thanks evermore, everywhere, to my heroine, Amanda.

I M A G E   C R E D I T S

11 t Chronicle/Alamy; 11 b © 50th Street Films/courtesy Everett Collection/Alamy; 12 t TOKUMA SHOTEN/Album/Alamy; 12 b Landmark Media/Alamy; 13 t Rischgitz/Getty Images; 13 b TKsdik8900 (Public domain); 15 l John Chillingworth/Picture Post/Getty Images; 15 r Bettmann/Getty Images; 16 Landmark Media/Alamy; 17 t The Book of Lost Things by John Connolly. Book cover of the Japanese edition (Sogensuiri Bunko, Tokyo Sogensha, translated by Shimon Tauchi, 2006).; 17 b TCD/Prod DB © Studio Ghibli - Toho Company/Alamy; 19 OPTIMUM RELEASING/All Star Picture Library/Alamy; 20 The Yomiuri Shimbun via AP Images/Alamy; 21 Gods, Demigods and Demons by Bernard Evslin (I.B. Tauris, 2006); 23 t © Patrice Cartier. All rights reserved 2025/Bridgeman Images; 23 b © Archives Charmet/Bridgeman Images; 24 t Chronicle/Alamy; 24 b Studio Ghibli/Photo 12/Alamy; 25 Archives du 7e Art/Studio Ghibli/Photo 12/Alamy; 26 San Diego Museum of Art/Edwin Binney 3rd Collection/Bridgeman Images; 27 tl © Archives Charmet/Bridgeman Images; 27 tr From the British Library archive/Bridgeman Images; 27 bl Photo © Photo Josse/Bridgeman Images; 27 br Historic Illustrations/PhotoStock-Israel/Alamy; 31 l GL Archive/Alamy; 31 r Historic Illustrations/PhotoStock-Israel/Alamy; 32 tl Pressens Bild/AFP via Getty Images; 32 tr © Gkids/courtesy Everett Collection//Alamy; 32 b Studio Ghibli/Photo 12/Alamy; 33 t can yalcin/Alamy; 33 b Jon Sparks/Alamy; 34 t FUJI TELEVISION/Allstar Picture Library Limited./Alamy; 34 b Archives du 7e Art/Studio Ghibli/Photo 12/Alamy; 37 l Le Petit Prince by Antoine de Saint-Exupéry (Gallimard, 1999); 37 r Terre des Hommes by Antoine de Saint-Exupéry (Gallimard, 1954); 38 t Studio Ghibli/Photo 12/Alamy; 38 bl piemags/archive/military/Alamy; 38 br ullstein bild/Getty Images; 41 Christie's Images/Bridgeman Images; 42 t Moviestore Collection Ltd/Alamy; 42 b Studio Ghibli/Photo 12/Alamy; 43 GL Archive/Alamy; 45 Gainew Gallery/Alamy; 46 l How Do You Live? by Genzaburō Yoshino (Penguin, 2023); 46 r The Yomiuri Shimbun via AP Images; 48–49 TCD/PProd DB © Studio Ghibli - Toho Company/Alamy; 53 t © Accessible Japan, taken by Jean and Justin Schroth; 53 b © Buena Vista Pictures/Courtesy Everett Collection/Alamy; 54–55 iStock Editorial/Getty Images Plus; 56 kpa Publicity Stills/United Archives GmbH/Alamy; 57 t From the collection of Steve Sundberg, OldTokyo.com; 57 b Disney Enterprises/Album/Alamy; 59 since1827/Shutterstock; 60–61 © Dimension Films/courtesy Everett Collection/Alamy; 62 l Journographie.com; 62 r yannick luthy/Alamy; 63 TOKUMA SHOTEN/Album/Alamy; 65 tl Hulton Archive/Getty Images; 65 tr Lupin III: The Castle of Cagliostro © Tokyo Movie Shinsha/Toho; 65 b stockex/Alamy; 66 t Feng Wei Photography/Getty Images; 66 b Studio Ghibli/Photo 12/Alamy; 67 Screen Archives/Getty Images; 69 t NCJ Archive/Mirrorpix/Getty Images; 69 b Keystone/Getty Images; 70 Laurie Noble/Getty Images; 71 t MIKE WALKER/Alamy; 71 b Studio Ghibli/Photo 12/Alamy; 72 t Michael Abid/mauritius images GmbH/Alamy; 72 b © 2004 Nibariki/PictureLux/The Hollywood Archive/Alamy; 77 tl © Paul Freeman/Bridgeman Images; 77 tr © Sainsbury Centre for Visual Arts/Robert and Lisa Sainsbury Collection/Bridgeman Images; 77 b Studio Ghibli/Photo 12/Alamy; 78 t Disney Enterprises/Album/Alamy; 78 b Disney Enterprises/Album/Alamy; 79 t Studio Ghibli/Photo 12/Alamy; 79 b Spirited Away © Studio Ghibli/Toho; 80 Masa Uemura/Alamy; 81 Studio Ghibli/Photo 12/Alamy; 83 PRESSENS BILD/AFP via Getty Images; 84 tl Horizon Images/Motion/Alamy; 84 tr Kyodo News Stills via Getty Images; 84 b Ponyo © Studio Ghibli/Toho; 87 From the British Library archive/Bridgeman Images; 88 t Kyodo Photo via Credit: Newscom/Alamy Live News; 88 b Madrid, Spain. 04th Apr, 2024. view of the Exhibition 'THE ART OF MANGA' at the COAM in Madrid, April 4, 2024 Spain Credit: Sipa US/Alamy Live News; 89 Nausicaa of the Valley of the Wind Anime Comics Vol.1. (Tokuma Shoten, 2003); 91 t RGR Collection/Alamy; 91 b My Neighbor Totoro © Studio Ghibli/Toho; 92 t © Walt Disney/courtesy Everett Collection Inc/Alamy ; 92 b © Buena Vista Pictures/Courtesy Everett Collection/Alamy; 93 Gift of Charles Stewart Smith, 1893, Metropolitan Museum of Art, New York; 97 Gift of Theodore De Witt, 1923, Metropolitan Museum of Art, New York; 98 t My Neighbor Totoro © Studio Ghibli/Toho; 98 b © 2004 Nibariki/PictureLux/The Hollywood Archive/Alamy ; 101 t Library of Congress; 101 b Galerie Bilderwelt/Getty Images); 102 t Studio Ghibli/Photo 12/Alamy; 102 b Howl's Moving Castle © Studio Ghibli/Toho; 103 Studio Ghibli/Photo 12/Alamy; 105 t © 50th Street Films/courtesy Everett Collection In/Alamy; 105 b kpa Publicity Stills/United Archives GmbH/Alamy; 106 t © Buena Vista Pictures/Courtesy Everett Collection Inc/Alamy; 106 b TOKUMA SHOTEN/Album/Alamy; 109 Everett Collection Inc/Alamy; 110 t TCD/Prod DB © NHK/Alamy; 110 b TCD/Prod DB © NHK/Alamy; 111 t TCD/Prod DB © NHK/Alamy; 111 b TCD/Prod DB © NHK/Alamy; 112 t Studio Ghibli/Photo 12/Alamy; 112 b © Touchstone Pictures/courtesy Everett Collection Inc/Alamy; 113 AP Photo/Koji Sasahara, File/Alamy;

117 © ADAGP, Paris and DACS, London 2025. Photo: © Israel Museum, Jerusalem/Gift of Harry Torczyner, New York/Bridgeman Images; 118 t Dessin réalisé pour une campagne de désensablement du Mont Saint-Michel, patronné par la Fondation de la Nature et de l'Environnement (INITIAL BD) © Jean Giraud Mœbius/Mœbius Production.; 118 b © Buena Vista/Allstar Picture Library Limited./Alamy; 119 Nicolas Guerin/Contour by Getty Images; 121 t Future Boy Conan © Nippon Animation; 121 b Future Boy Conan © Nippon Animation; 122 t Hakuhodo/Photo 12/Alamy; 122 b Future Boy Conan © Nippon Animation; 123 t Retro AdArchives/Alamy; 123 b The Incredible Tide by Alexander Key. Cover design by Jesse Hayes. Published by Open Road Media.; 125 The Asahi Shimbun via Getty Images; 126 Studio Ghibli/Photo 12/Alamy; 127 Rijksmuseum (CC0 1.0 Universal); 129 tl A Wizard of Earthsea by Ursula K. Le Guin (Puffin, 2010); 129 tr Archives du 7e Art/Studio Ghibli/Photo 12/Alamy; 129 b © Walt Disney Pictures/Courtesy: Everett Collection Inc/Alamy; 130 t beibaoke/Alamy; 130 b Mrk movie/Universal Images Group North America LLC/Alamy; 131 Pictures from History/Bridgeman Images; 135 Toei Doga/Photo 12/Alamy; 136 The Wind Rises © Studio Ghibli/Toho; 137 Photo 12/Alamy; 139 Fabrice Dall'Anese/Corbis via Getty Images; 140 t The Stapleton Collection/Bridgeman Images; 140 b Moviestore Collection Ltd/Alamy; 143 t Takehiko Suzuki/Associated Press/Alamy; 143 b Princess Mononoke © Studio Ghibli/Toho; 144 t Moviestore Collection Ltd/Alamy; 144 b Landmark Media/Alamy; 145 Studio Ghibli/Photo 12/Alamy; 147 tl © Buena Vista/courtesy Everett Collection Inc/Alamy; 147 tr 2019 TIFF/AFLO/Alamy Live News; 147 b TOKUMA SHOTEN/Album/Alamy; 148 tl Jean Baptiste Lacroix/WireImage/Getty Images; 148 tr The Yomiuri Shimbun via AP Images/Alamy; 148 b BJ Warnick/Newscom/Alamy; 153 Fleischer Studios/Album/Alamy; 154 t Pictorial Press Ltd/Alamy; 154 b A7A collection/Photo 12/Alamy; 155 A7A collection/Photo 12/Alamy; 156 Moviestore Collection Ltd/Alamy; 157 l A7A collection/Photo 12/Alamy; 157 r © Archives Charmet/Bridgeman Images; 159 t Gamma-Rapho/Getty Images; 159 b Les Films Paul Grimault/Photo 12/Alamy; 160 Les Films Paul Grimault/Photo 12/Alamy; 161 l Everett Collection Inc/Alamy; 161 r Buena Vista/AA Film Archive/Allstar Picture Library Ltd/Alamy; 163 t © Fairy Art Museum/Bridgeman Images; 163 b The Snow Queen © Soyuzmultfilm; 164 t kpa Publicity Stills/United Archives GmbH/Alamy; 164 b The Snow Queen © Soyuzmultfilm; 165 Pictures From History/Universal Images Group via Getty Images; 167 tl L'homme qui plantait des arbres by Jean Giono (Gallimard, 2018); 167 tr John Barr/Liaison/Hulton Archive/Getty Images; 167 b Hakuhodo/Photo 12/Alamy; 169 Kyodo News Stills via Getty Images; 170 t © Gkids/courtesy Everett Collection/Alamy; 170 b Shinchosha Company/Photo 12/Alamy; 171 Victor Fraile/Getty Images; 175 t Entertainment Pictures/Alamy; 175 b TCD/Prod DB © Studio Ghibli - Toho Company/Alamy; 176 t Moviestore Collection Ltd/Alamy; 176 b TOKUMA SHOTEN/Album/Alamy; 177 Photo 12/Alamy; 178 t Entertainment Pictures/Alamy; 178 b Everett Collection Inc/Alamy; 179 Studio Ghibli/Photo 12/Alamy; 181 t TOHO/Album/Alamy; 181 b Columbia/Allstar Picture Library Limited./Alamy; 182 t Toho/Atlaspix/Alamy; 182 b Moviestore Collection Ltd/Alamy; 183 t RKO/Allstar Picture Library Limited./Alamy; 183 b Everett Collection, Inc./Alamy; 185 t Archives du 7e Art/Photo 12/Alamy; 185 b The Wind Rises © Studio Ghibli/Toho; 187 tl Paramount Pictures/Photo 12/Alamy; 187 bl JT Vintage/Glasshouse Images/Alamy ; 187 r Album/Alamy; 188–189 Disney Enterprises/Album/Alamy; 190 Hum Images/Alamy; 191 Everett Collection Inc/Alamy; 193 t © STUDIO GHIBLI/BUENA VISTA HOME/Cinematic/Alamy; 193 b © MGM/FlixPix/Alamy; 194 t © STUDIO GHIBLI/BUENA VISTA HOME/Maximum Film/Alamy; 194 b TCD/Prod.DB © Akira Kurosawa Inc. - Warner Bros/Alamy ; 195 AP Photo/Koji Sasahara/Alamy; 199 t Metropolitan Museum of Art, New York; 199 b Collection Christophel/Alamy; 200 Night on the Galactic Railroad cover by Kenji Miyazawa (Kadokawa, 2012); 201 © Touchstone Pictures/courtesy Everett Collection/Alamy; 203 t © The Trustees of the British Museum; 203 b Princess Mononoke © Studio Ghibli/Toho; 204 The Asahi Shimbun via Getty Images; 207 t Metropolitan Museum of Art, New York; 207 b © Walt Disney Co./Courtesy Everett Collection Inc/Alamy; 208 t Metropolitan Museum of Art, New York; 208 b Spirited Away © Studio Ghibli/Toho; 210 t © Erich Lessing/Bridgeman Images; 210 b IanDagnall Computing/Alamy; 211 Studio Ghibli/Album/Alamy; 213 t © Bristol Museums, Galleries & Archives/Bridgeman Images; 213 b TCD/Prod DB © Fictive - NEOPA/Alamy; 214 Archives du 7e Art/Photo 12/Alamy; 215 Gkids/courtesy Everett Collection Inc/Alamy.

Quarto

First published in 2025 by Frances Lincoln,
an imprint of The Quarto Group.
One Triptych Place, London, SE1 9SH,
United Kingdom
T (0)20 7700 9000
www.Quarto.com

EEA Representation, WTS Tax d.o.o.,
Žanova ulica 3, 4000 Kranj, Slovenia
www.wts-tax.si

A catalogue record for this book is available
from the British Library.

ISBN 978-1-83600-481-3
Ebook ISBN 978-1-83600-482-0

10 9 8 7 6 5 4 3 2 1

Design by Intercity

Publisher Philip Cooper
Senior Commissioning Editor John Parton
Senior Editor Laura Bulbeck
Senior Designer Isabel Eeles
Senior Production Manager Alex Merrett

Printed in Guangdong, China TT062025

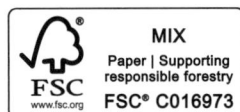

224

MIX
Paper | Supporting
responsible forestry
FSC
www.fsc.org
FSC® C016973